Discover Your calling purpose and ministry

to expand the Kingdom of God in the earth

TIM KURTZ

PUBLISHED BY
KINGDOM WORD PUBLICATIONS
ALBION, MICHIGAN 49224

Printed in the U.S.A

ISBN 978-0-9712916-2-1
Library of Congress Control Number: 2011912046

Unless otherwise noted, all scripture references are taken from the King James Version of the Bible.

Cover Design WRITERIGHTPRO PUBLISHING SERVICES
Cover Preparation ALBIONDESIGN
Professional Copy Edit Services by KINGDOMSCRIBE SERVICES

Table of Contents

KINGDOM WORD PUBLICATIONS is the publishing division of The Center for New Testament Church Development. Our mission is to produce and distribute quality materials that strengthen believers and assist them in planting and developing churches structured after New Testament patterns.

We pray that these materials will aid in equipping believers and help to lay firm foundations that exalt the Lord Jesus Christ as He builds His church and extends His Kingdom in the earth.

Learn more about how Jesus is building His Church – His way – with believers like you. Please Visit Our Website:

www.ntcdonline.org

Acknowledgments
So Many To Thank...

We are a reflection of those who have impacted our lives. A dedication or acknowledgement in a book is more than a public 'thank you'. In reality, it is the author's attempt to acknowledge that whatever success they may enjoy is attributable to the people who have influenced them. I remain on a quest to reach my highest potential in the Lord. I have learned that I cannot do it alone. I readily acknowledge that my place in this season is due to those who played a significant role in my journey. It would take another volume to thank them all.

First, I dedicate this book to my parents – the late Theodore and Lucille Kurtz. They had the foresight to keep me moving in a specific direction. They expected my best without compromise. They allowed me to error, and yet loved me in spite of my flaws. Momma was a prolific reader, Daddy was a hard worker. Together they were a strong thinking team whose wisdom was planted in my soul. I can only repay them for their love and direction by becoming the best that I can be.

Second, I dedicate this book to two specific pastors that I have served under – the late Reverend M. H. Wheeler and the late Superintendent Robert L. Brown. As a child, my parents saw to it that I was 'planted in the House of the Lord', specifically, Bethel Missionary Baptist Church. Pastor Wheeler created an atmosphere in Bethel that encouraged achievement and success.

As a young adult, the Lord set me in Grace Temple Church of God in Christ (1Corinthians 12:18). Under Pastor Brown I developed strength of mind to endure ministry and a resolve to live holy. He too provided a path for me to express myself musically and in ministry. Without question, both Pastor Wheeler and Pastor Brown gave me an opportunity to flourish (Psalms 92:13). My calling, purpose and ministry took root in these churches.

I appreciate my church family – New Life Ministries International. They are proof that my calling, purpose and ministry is being fulfilled. As they individually and corporately reach their destinies, it validates the vision the Lord gave me on the morning of December 15, 1991, *that they shall be the called 'trees of righteousness - the planting of the Lord, that He might be glorified!'* (Isaiah 61:3)

Finally, every book I write is made possible through the support of my wife – my soul mate – the love of my life, Carolyn. She knows the *real* me. In thirty-seven years of marriage, she has seen my peaks and my lows. She has enjoyed seasons of success and kept me close during times of failure and loss. It takes a strong and special woman to stand by a man in search of himself. I am so blessed to have her in my life.

To God be the glory for the things He has done!

Tim
July 2011

Calling, Purpose & Ministry
Getting Refocused

Every believer has a calling, a purpose and a ministry designed by God. But often, they seem difficult to find. When I first wrote this book in 2001 my intention was to help you identify God's calling, purpose and ministry for your life – and basically, that is still my focus. In the last nine plus years the Lord has taught me so much regarding the values and structure of His Church, and specifically, how your calling, purpose and ministry fits into it.

In the beginning God created the heaven and the earth. (Genesis 1:1)

In the beginning was the Word, and the Word was with God, and the Word was God. The same was in the beginning with God. All things were made by him; and without him was not any thing made that was made. (John 1:1-3)

And this gospel of the kingdom shall be preached in all the world for a witness unto all nations; and then shall the end come. (Matthew 24:14)

Then cometh the end, when he shall have delivered up the kingdom to God, even the Father; when he shall have put down all rule and all authority and power (1Corinthians 15:24)

Remember the former things of old: for I am God, and there is none else; I am God, and there is none like me, Declaring the end from the beginning, and from ancient times the things that are not yet done, saying, My counsel shall stand, and I will do all my pleasure: (Isaiah 46:9-10)

Scripture declares that you were chosen in Him from the foundation of the world (Ephesians 1:4). God has said He knows the plans He has for you with the full intent of bringing you to an *expected end* (Jeremiah 29:11). You are predestined to be conformed to the image of His Son, Jesus Christ (Romans 8:29).

The fact that God declared the end from the beginning reveals that this very moment you are in right now (while reading this book), was declared even before Genesis 1:1 was ever penned by Moses. You are located somewhere between *in the beginning* and *the declared end*.

2

However, do not lose sight of the fact that you are reading this book by choice. Yes, this moment was declared from the beginning, but the choice to be doing whatever you are doing is yours. This is important to understand. This moment is a point of alignment for you.

You are reading this book most likely because you are yearning to discover your calling, purpose and ministry. God knows the plans He has for you, but often you may feel that you have been left in the dark regarding those plans. You want to know God's will – therefore you read this seeking to line up with God's design for your life. It is in the process of coming into alignment with God's will that your calling, purpose and ministry are discovered.

Your calling exists. Your purpose was identified before the foundation of the world. Your ministry awaits your arrival. You just need to discover it. This is why this book was originally written in 2001, and it is why it has been updated now in 2011.

THE SECRET OF ASSIGNMENT

The familiar story of David and Goliath provides ten clear principles that will help you find God's calling, purpose and ministry for your life. David was destined to become the king of Israel, but how he handled the process from tending sheep to killing the giant paved the way for his ultimate destiny – to become king.

David killed the Philistine giant, but the story clearly reveals that his original mission had nothing to do with the giant. David was simply obeying his earthly father when the opportunity to confront Goliath was made possible. The path to becoming king began with an assignment. How he handled that assignment provides an opportunity for you to learn a valuable lesson.

Your destiny is often found in your current assignment. Your assignment does not have to have any obvious and direct connection to your ultimate calling. Many times what you have been instructed to do, becomes the birthing place for what God has called you to do. Within your calling, your purpose is realized. Your purpose has been prepared by God to function in a spiritual and or physical environment, which is your ministry. All of this begins with seemingly insignificant assignments. Often what you are assigned to do has very little to do with your destiny. Your assignment is the proving ground for your promotion.

David did not ascend to the throne immediately after Samuel anointed him. It was a grueling process of nearly thirteen years. Many miss their calling and purpose because they fail to understand the principle of accurately fulfilling their current assignment. They jump into what they believed to be their ministry without considering the purpose for their calling. They fail to understand the value of *process*. It is during process that calling and divine purposes are clarified.

Without clarification from the Holy Spirit, ministry will often be at the wrong place at the wrong time. As a consequence, the problems encountered are not the result of satanic attacks, but rather the result of being out of alignment with the will of the Father. This often results in disaster of hopes and dreams, and at times permanent damage to a person's spiritual life.

I encourage you to enjoy this moment. God wants you to walk into His calling, His purpose and His ministry for your life (Jeremiah 1:5). The significance of walking in alignment in the Kingdom is critical. Seek Him to become totally aligned with His calling for you. Learn His purpose which causes all things to work together in your behalf (Romans 8:28). Rest assured there is a place for His ministry in you to flourish (Psalms 92:13)

CALLING, PURPOSE AND MINISTRY

I am often asked, "How do you know what you are called to do?" For years I tried to answer this question to the best of my ability. Often I would point the individual towards their talents, passions and skills. I would give them my personal testimony. I would recite stories of local and national successes and some key points of their journey to the top, but often I felt my answers were inadequate.

We all are created uniquely by God (Psalms 139:14). Each of us has a divine calling, within a defined purpose for a specific ministry (Ephesians 4:1). It is mind boggling to think that literally billions of people are all crafted individually by God with such unique specificity.

Several years ago I was preparing a syllabus for a leadership course. My intent was to use the story of David and Goliath to teach about overcoming giants. As I meditated on this story, I realized that Goliath was not David's reason for being on the battlefield. Goliath was simply the door to his destiny to become king of Israel. The more I studied David; I realized that his story revealed a key to the question of "How do I know my calling?"

Killing the giant was not David's destiny. It was a clear stage he had to go through to get there. Likewise, while obeying your current assignment, you may be faced with giants that will attempt to stop you. You must kill the giant in order to move to your next place – which may simply be another assignment.

Throughout this book I will refer to callings, purposes and ministries. All three are closely linked, but each has a significant distinction. Your understanding of these distinctions will help you to personally discover your place in life. Once you discover God's plan for your life, it will produce a confidence in you that nothing can diminish.

THE ETERNAL PURPOSE
AND THE KINGDOM MANDATE

There is one purpose given to the Church. It is the mandate that was given to man in the Garden of Eden, and reinforced by Jesus Christ throughout His life on earth and after His resurrection. The sole purpose was encased in the Kingdom of God. It is the Kingdom Mandate.

In the Garden, man was commanded *to be fruitful, to multiply, to replenish and to subdue the earth* (Genesis 1:28). This is the original mandate given to man. It is the mandate to release the authority of God into the earth realm. It is the mandate to expand the Kingdom of God into territories decimated by satan.

Man was designed to have dominion in the earth realm, but he rebelled and sinned against God. This failure set in motion a divine plan that would redeem man and restore him on the path towards fulfilling the original mandate. By the blood of Jesus Christ, man has been redeemed. Yet, the fulfillment of the Kingdom Mandate is still being actuated in the earth realm (Daniel 7:27; 1Corinthians 15:24; Revelation 11:15). This is central to understanding what you are called to do, your purpose for doing it and where you will accomplish it.

For three and a half years, Jesus preached and demonstrated the message of the Kingdom of God (Matthew 4:23; 9:35). In the plan of God, Jesus became the sacrifice and source of redemption for all mankind. The cross became the catalyst for establishing God's plan in the earth permanently (1Corinthians 1:18; Colossians 1:20). But Jesus did not remain on the cross. He was buried three days in a borrowed tomb. On the surface, it appeared that all was lost to man, but it was during those three days that our eternal victory was sealed and our earthly capacities were reinforced.

On the third day Jesus rose from the dead. For forty days He reinforced the message of the Kingdom of God. As He ascended back into heaven, He did two significant things. First, He gave the marching orders for His Church to go into all the world and make disciples of every nation (Matthew 28:19). This was not a suggestion, but a reiteration of the original mandate to be fruitful, to multiply, to replenish and subdue the earth.

> *And to make all men see what is the fellowship of the mystery, <u>which from the beginning of the world hath been hid in God</u>, who created all things by Jesus Christ: To the intent that now unto the principalities and powers in heavenly places <u>might be known by the church</u> the manifold wisdom of God, <u>According to the eternal purpose which he purposed in Christ Jesus our Lord</u> (Ephesians 3:9-11)*

The eternal purpose of God was set in His mind before anything was created. It was released in the earth realm when He gave the command to be fruitful, multiply, replenish the earth and subdue it. It will be fulfilled when Jesus submits the Kingdom to the Father, and it is declared that the kingdoms of this world are now the Kingdom of our God and His Christ.

Throughout this book I will regularly remind you of the eternal purpose of God, the Kingdom Mandate, which is to subdue all kingdoms under the Kingdom of God through Jesus Christ and to reclaim and redeem the earth and its inhabitants from its satanic intruder (Daniel 2:44; 4:3; Luke 1:32-33; John 3:16-17; 1Corinthians 15:24; Revelation 11:15).

THE WORK OF MINISTRY

Let's briefly turn our attention to ministry – specifically the *work of ministry*. When I first heard the term 'work of ministry' I assumed it referred to the various tasks we do around the church. Teaching Sunday school, serving as an usher, singing in the choir, operating the sound and audio equipment, and working in the nursery were all tasks that I believe constituted the 'work of ministry'. These are wonderful helps in the church structure as we know it today. However, when the Apostle Paul wrote this to the church at Ephesus, none of these activities existed. Therefore, the work of ministry clearly has to be something totally different.

> *Go ye therefore, and teach all nations, baptizing them in the name of the Father, and of the Son, and of the Holy Ghost: Teaching them to observe all things whatsoever I have commanded you: and, lo, I am with you alway, even unto the end of the world. Amen. (Matthew 28:19-20)*

> *For whom he did foreknow, he also did predestinate to be conformed to the image of his Son, that he might be the firstborn among many brethren. (Romans 8:29)*

The *work of ministry* finds its foundation in the highest operational policy of the Kingdom, which is to make disciples of all nations. The work of ministry is tasks done specifically for the benefit of God's purpose. If what we do does not line up with God's purposes, then our activities are no more than mundane religious activity.

Comprehending the *work of ministry* is the beginning of understanding your specific calling, purpose and ministry.

UNIVERSAL NATURE OF ALL CALLINGS

The work of ministry exposes the *universal nature* of everyone's calling. In essence, the nature of each of our callings is exactly the same. Your basic calling is the same as mine. Let me share with you the nature of my calling:

I AM CALLED TO INSURE THAT YOUR CALLING AND MINISTRY IS FULFILLED.

Let that sink in for a moment. The nature of your calling is exactly the same. You are called to insure that someone else's calling and ministry is fulfilled in the earth. Your ministry discipline may be different from mine, but the nature of that calling is exactly the same as mine – to insure that someone else's calling is fulfilled.

The work of ministry can be summarized into making disciples of all nations. If making disciples is not at the root of your calling, you may need to reassess it. To make disciples is the policy of the Kingdom of God. Making disciples is the primary work of ministry.

> Often what you are assigned to do has very little to do with your destiny. It is only the proving ground for your promotion.

To supplement your efforts, Jesus gave gifts to men in the form of apostles, prophets, evangelists, pastors and teachers. Scripture makes it clear that their role is to equip the saints for the work of ministry. They are given by God to develop you. It is through the *work of ministry* (making disciples) that your specific calling and ministry in conjunction with the eternal purpose is revealed.

We must esteem others more than ourselves (Philippians 2:3). We are to exhort one another daily (Hebrews 3:13; 10:25). We are to be kind and prefer one another (Romans 12:10). My *calling or discipline* may be apostolic. Yours may be prophetic. Someone else may be pastoral, while others may be teachers. One person may be a carpenter while another may be a musician. Your calling or discipline[1] is a function in the overall body of Christ. Your calling or discipline is no greater or lesser than any other calling or discipline. These are simply specific callings and disciplines entrusted to an individual to serve someone else. This is universal for all believers.

As an apostle, I must esteem, exhort, be kind to, and prefer others over myself. Prophets must esteem, exhort, be kind to and prefer others over themselves. Evangelist, Pastors and Teachers must esteem, exhort, be kind to and prefer others over themselves. No one is to be self-serving. Regardless of the calling or discipline you have been entrusted with by God, your basic calling is to allow God to use it to insure that someone else's purpose is fulfilled. Your calling is not given to you for personal gain.

---

[1] The terms *calling and discipline* will be used interchangeably throughout this book.

DEFINING PERSONAL CALLING

People often think of 'a calling' as the spiritual gifts they have (i.e. preaching, missionary work, etc.). Callings are not necessarily spiritual in nature. God uses people in all walks of life to advance His Kingdom and to serve others. Therefore, to limit callings to the activities done in a church setting is incorrect.

We tend to separate callings from careers. This usually stems from our spiritualization and secularization of the two. Our lives are often divided into the sacred from the secular. We have created a firm invisible line between our activities '*in the world*' and our activities '*in the church*'.

Unfortunately, there are laws and regulations that reinforce this division. In the government there are laws that attempt to separate church and state. In business, there are regulations in many work places that prohibit religious activities. The result is that our kingdom influence is suppressed – which is exactly what satan desires.

As our understanding of the Kingdom of God increases, we are learning that what was previously considered a secular career may actually be a divine placement by the Holy Spirit to perpetuate the purposes of God in the earth. In other words, a carpenter directed by the Holy Spirit has the same value in the Kingdom as any apostle, prophet, evangelist, pastor or teacher. What may be considered a secular career may in fact be the '*calling*' one has received from God. This is a critical truth to understand.

Having then gifts differing according to the grace that is given to us, whether prophecy, let us prophesy according to the proportion of faith; Or ministry, let us wait on our ministering: or he that teacheth, on teaching; Or he that exhorteth, on exhortation: he that giveth, let him do it with simplicity; he that ruleth, with diligence; he that sheweth mercy, with cheerfulness. Let love be without dissimulation. Abhor that which is evil; cleave to that which is good. Be kindly affectioned one to another with brotherly love; in honour preferring one another; (Romans 12:6-10)

...walk worthy of the vocation wherewith ye are called...(Ephesians 4:1)

Calling is defined as the specific thing, skill or talent that God has given to you. Generally we use the term 'calling' to describe a particular discipline an individual may be divinely or naturally proficient in. It is a discipline. There is no limit to what this may be. For some it may be music. For another it may be sports. Some may work with youth or senior citizens. It may be business. You could be prophetic or pastoral. You may be a teacher of the Word, an evangelist or possibly both. The variations are unlimited, but should always be understood to be a function in the Body of Christ.

Individual callings or disciplines are not unique. Many people can do the same thing. The world is filled with musicians, preachers, doctors, lawyers, carpenters and the like. There are over fifty pastors in my city. There are hundreds of pastors in my county. There are thousands of pastors in our state. There are millions of pastors in this country. We err in believing we are exclusive in our calling.

Elijah had a pity party. He thought that he was the only one called to do what he was doing. God made it clear to him that he had seven thousand who had not bowed to Baal (1Kings 19:18). Likewise, your calling may be unique for your area, but rest assured, you are not the only one called to do what you do.

DEFINING PERSONAL PURPOSE

What makes your calling or discipline unique? I believe the answer is found in understanding God's Eternal Purpose as it relates to your specific purpose.

> To the intent that now unto the principalities and powers in heavenly places might be known <u>by the church</u> the manifold wisdom of God, <u>according to the eternal purpose which he purposed in Christ Jesus our Lord</u> (Ephesians 3:10)

> And we know that all things work together for good to them that love God, <u>to them who are the called according to his purpose.</u> (Romans 8:28)

Paul taught that the wisdom of God would be revealed to the spirit realm by the church. That has been God's plan throughout eternity. I will not cover some of the misconceptions regarding the values and structure of the New Testament Church in this book.[2] What you need to understand is God's eternal purpose for His church.

---

[2] NO LONGER CHURCH AS USUAL *Restoring first century values and structure to the 21st Century Church* © 2010 T. Lemoss Kurtz Kingdom Word Publications

Anything the church pursues must be enveloped in the divine eternal purpose of the Father – WHICH IS TO RECLAIM AND REDEEM THE EARTH AND ITS INHABITANTS FROM ITS SATANIC INTRUDER.

Then cometh the end, when he shall have delivered up the kingdom to God, even the Father; <u>when he shall have put down all rule and all authority and power</u>. <u>For he must reign, till he hath put all enemies under his feet</u>. The last enemy that shall be destroyed is death. <u>For he hath put all things under his feet</u>. But when he saith <u>all things</u> are put under him, it is manifest that he is excepted, which did put <u>all things</u> under him. And when all things shall be subdued unto him, then shall the Son also himself be subject unto him that put all things under him, <u>that God may be all in all</u>. (1Corinthians 15:24-28)

And the seventh angel sounded; and there were great voices in heaven, saying, <u>The kingdoms of this world are become the kingdoms of our Lord, and of his Christ</u>; and he shall reign for ever and ever. (Revelation 11:15)

> Everything we do must find its root in the ultimate purpose of God to reclaim the earth. Our individual purposes must reflect our part in the fulfillment of His universal purpose.

Too many churches are spiritual franchises stamping out manmade ideologies in the Name of the Lord. They are led by well meaning religionist that embrace humanistic vision statements without ever touching the purpose of God. They have not understood that God's ultimate purpose is not the size and popularity of their church, but rather the dominion of the Creator expressed through them.

The Church is responsible for the *corporate implementation* of God's purpose in the earth. The Church however, is made up of individuals. Each person is a lively stone who with other believers create a spiritual house for the Lord (1Peter 2:5). Each person is a fellow citizen with other saints and the household of God, built on the foundation of apostles and prophets with Jesus Christ being the chief cornerstone, and who are built together as a holy temple of the Lord and habitation of God (Ephesians 2:19-22).

Each of us are members of a universal body fitly joined together with other believers with a personal discipline that strengthens other believers (Ephesians 4:16). Our personal discipline or calling has been given to us to use within God's eternal purpose. It was the Godhead who originally created man. "Let *us* make man...to have dominion" underscores the Divine Intent of the Father, Son and Spirit to create a being in the earth for His purpose (Genesis 1:26).

Let's regress for a moment. Everything we do must find its root in the ultimate purpose of God to reclaim the earth. Our individual purposes must reflect our part in the fulfillment of His universal purpose. What we do individually must reflect His global purpose. This is critical to understand going forward in this book. Never believe that your specific purpose is detached from God's ultimate and universal purpose.

DEFINING YOUR MINISTRY

Calling is the specific thing that you do. Many are called and can do the same thing that you do, but your calling is defined by your purpose. Purpose is defined by *how* your calling is used to serve people in the purposes of God. Ministry is defined by *strategy and location*.

Beyond the specific calling and its purpose is where it will be implemented. This is important. You need a specific and divine strategy to accomplish the purposes of the Lord. You need to know where you are to execute your work. What will work in Albion, Michigan may have no effect in the Bronx, New York. What may be effective in the inner city may be totally rejected in suburban areas. The Lord is not looking for duplication. He expects effectiveness.

> *And when they were come, and had gathered the church together, they rehearsed all that God had done with them, and how he had opened the door of faith unto the Gentiles (Acts 14:27)*

> *Furthermore, when I came to Troas to [preach] Christ's gospel, and a door was opened unto me of the Lord (2Corinthians 2:12)*

> *Withal praying also for us, that God would open unto us a door of utterance, to speak the mystery of Christ, for which I am also in bonds (Colossians 4:3)*

Gbile Akanni of Gboko, Nigeria teaches about three specific doors. It is vital that we pray that God opens these doors for us. This book will not detail each door, but a summary of all three will help you to understand them – specifically the door of ministry.

The door of utterance is opened to you so that you can articulate your purpose clearly to those God sends you to (Colossians 4:3). God opens a door of faith so that those you are sent to will receive your message (Acts 14:27). Finally, the door of ministry is when the Lord opens up a place or people for you to serve His purposes (2Corinthians 2:12).

We have the same gospel. We use the same Gifts of the Spirit. We have the same ministry offices available to us. But we are given different strategies for different territories. Peter and Paul were both apostles. Peter's purpose was to the Jews and Paul's purpose was to the Gentiles (Galatians 2:7-8; Ephesians 3:1; 2Timothy 1:11). Peter's ministry was primarily located in Jerusalem, whereas Paul ministered throughout Asia Minor.

Finally, your calling, your purpose and your ministry is discovered through God's process. You cannot bypass process and expect to be successful. The story of David and Goliath reveals ten principles that will help you to walk through God's process – the process that will help you discover your calling, your purpose and your ministry.

YOU DON'T FIT – YOU CONTRIBUTE

When I first made the statement 'you don't fit – you contribute', there were some who thought I was refuting Ephesians 4:16 that asserts we are a body fitly joined together. I believe my statement actually brings clarity to what scripture says.

There are many gifts lying dormant in the church because only a select few are ever given the opportunity to use what God has given them. Many are clamoring to fill the limited positions at the top of our religious hierarchal church systems. They are vying to fit into a system rather than contribute to the purposes of the Father.

> *But speaking the truth in love, may grow up into him in all things, which is the head, even Christ: From whom the whole body fitly joined together and compacted by that which every joint supplieth, according to the effectual working in the measure of every part, maketh increase of the body unto the edifying of itself in love. (Ephesians 4:15,16)*

The church should reflect a body fitly or accurately joined together. You need to understand that in the Body of Christ, *you don't fit* (in the Westernized sense of the word) - *you contribute!* You are vital to the success of the whole body. The scripture declares that we are *fitly joined* together *with every joint supplying the whole body.* The Weymouth Translation records Ephesians 4:16 this way:

Dependent on Him, the whole body – its various parts closely fitting and firmly adhering to one another – grows by the aid of every contributory ligament, with power proportioned to the need of each individual part, so as to build itself up with a spirit of love.

Your calling becomes unique and necessary when it is used to fulfill eternal purposes. You are significant in the Kingdom when you serve to build the whole body. Provision and resources will be provided to anyone who lines up with the eternal purposes of the Lord (Romans 8:28).

Function trumps status in the Kingdom of God. Who you are has more value than what you do. But what you do should reflect who God has declared you to be (Jeremiah 1:5). In the next chapter we will discuss hierarchy in greater detail. Later, I will discuss in more detail the concept of contributing to the Body of Christ. Yes, the bible teaches that we are 'fitly' joined together, but it goes on to say that every part of the body contributes to the health of the whole body (Ephesians 4:16).

Usually when a person speaks of their calling, they inevitably describe what they do in the church. They have found a place to fit in. Too often their service is for the benefit of the church organization rather than the Body of Christ. They volunteer for programs that the church organization offers. They serve on committees for the perpetuity of the church organization. They become active in events that bolster the image of the church organization. All this is done while there are those around them are losing their homes, getting divorced, going bankrupt and facing life altering calamities. The church maintains a healthy image but the people in it are dying financially and emotionally.

Let me assert that some of the programs offered by these churches are targeted to meet needs in the community. But if the church organization fails, the programs ceases. I believe a person with a calling will serve regardless. They may garner volunteers to help them, but do not allow lack of support to hamper their work. They may raise funds but they move forward with whatever resources they have.

Those who claim to be in ministry usually imply they have a higher calling – a divine grace that sets them above other believers. It is as though their calling from God made them spiritual experts by osmosis. In our hierarchal thinking, we usually accept the spiritual superiority of those called in ministry over those called to serve as an usher. Their messages are often laced with *'how to be a good servant of the Lord'*. This usually means, avoid blatant sin as not to embarrass the church, serve in some capacity in the organization and of course give liberally to support the 'work'.

We have seen the results of this mindset. People who serve the needs of the organization that lack character, morals and basic Christian beliefs. We overlook adultery because the individual has the skills to organize a particular department. We overlook a woman shacking with her boyfriend because she has the kind of voice we want in our choir or praise team. We promote a man based on his charisma rather than his holiness – all to bolster the image of the organization.

Scripture teaches that each one of us contribute to the overall health of the Body of Christ. What you and I do is not ranked in order of importance, but rather how we contribute to the growth and health of the Body of Christ in the earth. I am an apostle, teacher and writer. Each of these are functions in the Body of Christ, none of which make me greater (or lesser) than any other believer serving the Body of Christ in their callings.

For as the body is one, and hath many members, and all the members of that one body, being many, are one body: so also is Christ. For by one Spirit are we all baptized into one body, whether we be Jews or Gentiles, whether we be bond or free; and have been all made to drink into one Spirit. For the body is not one member, but many. (1Corinthians 12:12-14)

But now hath God set the members every one of them in the body, as it hath pleased him. (1Corinthians 12:18)

Nay, much more those members of the body, which seem to be more feeble, are necessary: And those members of the body, which we think to be less honourable, upon these we bestow more abundant honour; and our uncomely parts have more abundant comeliness. (1Corinthians 12:22)

For our comely parts have no need: but God hath tempered the body together, having given more abundant honour to that part which lacked: That there should be no schism in the body; but that the members should have the same care one for another. (1Corinthians 12:24-25)

And we beseech you, brethren, to know them which labour among you, and are over you in the Lord, and admonish you; And to esteem them very highly in love for their work's sake. And be at peace among yourselves. (1Thessalonians 5:12-13)

Obey them that have the rule over you, and submit yourselves: for they
watch for your souls, as they that must give account, that they may do it
with joy, and not with grief: for that is unprofitable for you. (Hebrews
13:17)

THE EXPRESSIONS OF GOD

I am writing this near the close of a month long sabbatical I took from teaching and preaching. During this time the Lord has spoken many truths into my spirit. One is particularly apropos to where this book will lead you.

For several days the Lord has taught me about how He is expressed. Our ability to accurately see, hear and to walk in sync with Him is directly linked to us comprehending how He expresses Himself.

There are three dimensions of His expression – *His Power, His Person and His Potential.* He is Father, Son and Holy Spirit. From the Father we discover the expression of His Power. The Son expresses His Person and the Holy Spirit expresses God's Earthly Potential.

For this cause I bow my knees unto the Father of our Lord Jesus Christ,
Of whom the whole family in heaven and earth is named, That he would
grant you, according to the riches of his glory, to be strengthened with
might by his Spirit in the inner man; <u>*That Christ may dwell in your*</u>
<u>*hearts by faith; that ye, being rooted and grounded in love, May be able*</u>

to comprehend with all saints what is the breadth, and length, and depth, and height; And to know the love of Christ, which passeth knowledge, that ye might be filled with all the fulness of God. (Ephesians 3:14-19)

First, *the greatest expression of God's Power is His Kingdom*. You cannot see the Kingdom and not recognize that He rules over it. In other words, He will always be greater than your perception of His Kingdom. When Moses asked God to see His face, God allowed all of His goodness to pass before Moses (Exodus 33:19). In God's Kingdom there is goodness, power, authority and dominion (Romans 14:17; James 1:17). Moses could see the vastness of God through His goodness, and by being accurately positioned behind the Rock (Jesus Christ).

The Kingdom of God overshadows all other kingdoms. His eternal purpose in Christ, the Rock is the ultimate dominance of His Kingdom over all others (Daniel 7:27; 1Corinthians 10:1-4; 1Corinthians 15:24; Revelation 11:5). The imposition of the Kingdom of Heaven into the earth realm is His articulated desire (Matthew 6:10). He has chosen to give the Kingdom to believers (Matthew 16:19; Luke 12:32). He has strategically planted the Kingdom within us, where the effects of the world cannot easily reach it (Luke 17:20-21).

There was a man of the Pharisees, named Nicodemus, a ruler of the Jews: The same came to Jesus by night, and said unto him, Rabbi, we know that thou art a teacher come from God: for no man can do these miracles that thou doest, except God be with him. Jesus answered and said unto him,

Verily, verily, I say unto thee, <u>Except a man be born again, he cannot see</u>
<u>the kingdom of God</u> (John 3:1).

Nicodemus came to Jesus by night and in his Pharisee mindset declared Jesus as a teacher come from God. He had no problem seeing God's superiority over Jesus. However, Jesus responded by pointing Nicodemus to an accurate view of God's Kingdom.

The Pharisee's view of God and their environment was anthropomorphic. They were extremely limited in their sight by interpreting what they saw in human terms. Jesus directed Nicodemus's sight towards the Kingdom of God. Nicodemus measured Jesus' power by his relationship to God. Jesus always measured God's power by the expression of His Kingdom.

... For thine is the kingdom, and the power, and the glory, for ever. Amen
(Matthew 6:13).

Again, the kingdom of heaven is like unto treasure hid in a field; the
which when a man hath found, he hideth, and for joy thereof goeth and
selleth all that he hath, and buyeth that field. Again, the kingdom of
heaven is like unto a merchant man, seeking goodly pearls: Who, when he
had found one pearl of great price, went and sold all that he had, and
bought it (Matthew 13:44-46)

Then said he, Unto what is the kingdom of God like? and whereunto shall
I resemble it? It is like a grain of mustard seed, which a man took, and

cast into his garden; and it grew, and waxed a great tree; and the fowls of the air lodged in the branches of it. (Luke 13:18-19)

It is not until you comprehend the vastness of the Kingdom that you will thoroughly understand the power of God that is resident in you.

God has entrusted the Kingdom to His Son Jesus Christ. He rules over the Kingdom. He is our access to everything the Kingdom has to offer us on earth. If your view of the Kingdom is small, your perception of God and your personal capacity to be effective will be small. Likewise, if your view of the Kingdom is huge, then your perception of God and your personal capacity will match what you see. In either case, your analysis of the Kingdom reflects your assessment of God Himself. This may be why Jesus spent so much time teaching the Kingdom. Over and over he stated, *"The Kingdom of Heaven is like..."*. Through carefully crafted parables He would teach various dimensions of the Kingdom of God. The greatest expression of God's Power is His Kingdom.

Second, *the greatest expression of God's Person, is love.* Jesus Christ is the express image of God, and God is love (Hebrews 1:3; 1John 4:8). Jesus Christ was sent as an expression of God's love. God loved the world so much He sent His us His only Son (John 3:16).

Everything God does is motivated by love. When He blesses, it is motivated by love (1John 4:19). When He chastens and rebukes, it is motivated by love (Hebrews 12:6; Revelation 3:19). His judgment is motivated by love (Psalms 11:7). Even His ownership of vengeance is motivated by love of His people (Isaiah 43:4; 49:25; 54:17). Our earth bound view of love often misses the truth of God's love towards us (1John 3:1).

In the Garden of Eden, *First Adam* was given a mandate to be fruitful, to multiply, to replenish the earth and subdue it. Each of these commands collectively reflects a dimension of God's love released in the earth through man.

To *be fruitful* reflects an accurate dimension of *internal-love*. This is not the distorted and perverted self-love exhibited by the world (Philippians 2:21; 2Timothy 3:2). Correct *internal-love* is the inward recognition of God as the source of love in you. It is acknowledging that human love is no match for the love of God in us. Human love is self-serving, even when outward actions appear legitimate (Luke 6:21-36).

The love of God has filled our hearts through the Holy Spirit which was given us (Romans 5:5 *Twentieth Century New Testament*). Internal-love is recognizing that our capacity to love is through Him, and Him alone. Human love is limited to realms of the soul and flesh. *Internal-love* is recognizing that your existence is to please Him – and Him alone.

I am the true vine, and my Father is the husbandman. Every branch in me that beareth not fruit he taketh away: and every branch that beareth fruit, he purgeth it, that it may bring forth more fruit. Now ye are clean through the word which I have spoken unto you. Abide in me, and I in

you. As the branch cannot bear fruit of itself, except it abide in the vine;
no more can ye, except ye abide in me. I am the vine, ye are the branches:
He that abideth in me, and I in him, the same bringeth forth much fruit:
for without me ye can do nothing. If a man abide not in me, he is cast
forth as a branch, and is withered; and men gather them, and cast them
into the fire, and they are burned. If ye abide in me, and my words abide
in you, ye shall ask what ye will, and it shall be done unto you. Herein is
my Father glorified, that ye bear much fruit; so shall ye be my disciples
(John 15:1-8).

We are commanded to be fruitful. Healthy fruit requires a source of nourishment. Jesus declared that He is the True Vine. It is impossible to bear fruit that is pleasing to Him without being attached to Him – the True Vine. He is the source of nourishment and life for all fruit attached to Him.

Jesus declared that our Father has no tolerance for fruitlessness. Those who do not bear fruit are cut off and burned, and every fruit-bearing branch is purged in order for it to bring forth more fruit. Jesus makes it clear that it is absolutely impossible to produce fruit without Him.

All fruit carries a seed within it that has the capacity to reproduce more fruit (Genesis 1:11-12). We have been born again of an incorruptible seed – Jesus Christ (1Peter 1:23). If this incorruptible seed does not germinate within us, no fruit of value will be produced. The only way for it to germinate, is for us to die to self-love. We must die to self-love in order for the incorruptible seed to take root and bear fruit in our life. Dying to self-love acknowledges the *Internal-love* given to us by God to produce fruit in the earth. (Galatians 2:20; Ephesians 1:4; 2Corinthians 4:5-7).

Accurate *internal-love* is reflected in how you treat others. If you have a distorted view of God's love resident in you, your treatment of others will be tainted. You can only love others to the extent that you accurately love yourself (James 2:8).

How do you accurately love yourself? You love yourself by denying yourself, taking up your cross daily and following Jesus (Luke 9:23). You love yourself by knowing that in Jesus you live, move, and have your very being (Acts 17:28). You love yourself by recognizing that God sent Jesus into the world that we might live through Him (1John 4:9). The only way to love yourself is to decrease so that He may increase, for without Him we are nothing (John 3:30; 15:5; Philippians 4:13). You can love yourself by recognizing that you are ineradicably linked to the love of God (Romans 8:35-39).

The first command in the Kingdom Mandate is to be fruitful. The second command is to *multiply*. To be fruitful is the expression of God's love *internally*. To multiply requires the love of God to be expressed *externally*. Jesus capsulated the transition between being fruitful and multiplying when He answered the lawyer who tried to test him.

Then one of them, which was a lawyer, asked him a question, tempting him, and saying, Master, which is the great commandment in the law? Jesus said unto him, <u>Thou shalt love the Lord thy God with all thy heart,</u>

and with all thy soul, and with all thy mind. This is the first and great *commandment. And the second is like unto it, Thou shalt love thy* *neighbour as thyself.* On these two commandments hang all the law and the prophets (Matthew 22:35-40)

A seed that does not produce fruit is useless (John 12:24). Our love for our neighbor is a direct reflection of our accurate love of our selves. If I love myself incorrectly, I cannot minister to you accurately. If my internal view is imbalanced, my interaction with you will reflect my internal flaws. That is why we must allow the love of God to flow through us, rather than try to muster up an artificial humanistic religious love that is of little or no value to others (Galatians 2:20).

We love our neighbors as God loves us. God commends His own love toward us, in that while we were yet sinners, Christ died for us (Romans 5:8 World English Bible). We then must love our neighbors the same way God loves us (John 13:34; 15:12; Ephesians 5:2). Husbands are specifically commanded to love their wives as Christ loved the church (Ephesians 5:25). Jesus was sent into the world because of God's love (John 3:16-17). Jesus sends us into the world as His ambassadors of life (Matthew 5:14; John 8:12). The foundation of *multiplying* is to plant God's love into others. We are commanded to go into all the world and make disciples of all nations (Matthew 28:19-20).

The biblical concept is to multiply – not divide. A single fruit has within seed that can produce multiple fruit. A single fruit has the potential of an entire orchard within it. We understand that the seed is within the fruit, and that it produces after its own kind.

> *And God said, Let the earth bring forth grass, the herb yielding seed, and the fruit tree yielding fruit after his kind, whose seed is in itself, upon the earth: and it was so. And the earth brought forth grass, and herb yielding seed after his kind, and the tree yielding fruit, whose seed was in itself, after his kind: and God saw that it was good (Genesis 1:11-12).*

> *Of his own will begat he us with the word of truth, that we should be a kind of firstfruits of his creatures (James 1:18).*

You cannot help but recognize the connection between the seed and the multiplication of fruit. Fruit produces after its own kind. An apple (fruit) has the capacity within it (seed) to produce an orchard of apples. A tomato (fruit) has the capacity within it (seed) to produce a full garden of tomatoes. Every believer (fruit) has within them the word of truth, Jesus Christ (seed) to produce more believers.

This leads to the third component of the Kingdom Mandate which is to *replenish the earth* (Genesis 1:28). Replenishing reveals God's love for His creation. We replenish the earth by filling it with more people reflecting the Lord Jesus Christ.

Agri-terminology is found throughout all of scripture. Planting, sowing, reaping, and harvesting have become the typological language that helps us to understand the organic movement of God, His people and purposes in the earth.

Replenishing the earth has a two-fold meaning. To replenish is first to replace something that has been depleted. Every time you go grocery shopping, you are *replenishing* your cabinets with fresh food because you have depleted your previous supply. To replenish also means *to fill*. In Genesis 1:28, the Hebrew word *male'* (pronounced maw-lay) is often translated as *fill, full, fulfilled, and filled*. Peppered throughout scripture, how this word is translated gives us a greater understanding of the ancient understanding of what it means to fill or be filled.

Other words translated from male' include *satisfied* (Exodus 15:9), *consecrate* (Exodus 29:9), *to set* (Exodus 35:33), *took* (Leviticus 9:17), *wholly* (Deuteronomy 1:36), *presume* (Esther 7:5), *fenced* (2Samuel 23:7), *confirm* (1Kings 1:14), *expired* (1Chronicles 17:11), and *gather* (Jeremiah 51:11). Each of these words implicitly suggests bringing something to a full state of being. They implicitly describe an act of *leaving no room for anything else*. Even the word *consecrate* as found in Exodus 29:9 means to 'fill the hand'. To be specific, consecration in this context would mean that a person would be so full of the things of God, that there would be no room for anything else.

What does this mean to us today?

We are commanded to '*replenish the earth*'. If we are accurate in our obedience, then every territory we touch would be filled with Kingdom influence. Every gathering of believers should be *consecrated*. They should be *wholly, fenced in* and *set* in their minds that the Kingdom is their only message, and the mandate of the Kingdom is their sole mission. Every unsaved and distressed person that consecrated believers touch should have it *confirmed* in their spirit that the Kingdom of our Lord Jesus Christ is the only viable option for their deliverance. The effect of replenishing would be that the kingdoms of this world would become the Kingdom of our God (Revelation 11:15).

Finally, we are to subdue the earth. This is to stand firm against anything that opposes the purposes of God. This begins *internally* with each believer when we cast down incorrect imaginations and bring our thoughts under subjection. Then we have the capacity to readily revenge all acts of disobedient forces because of the accuracy flowing in us.

> *For the weapons of our warfare are not carnal, but mighty through God to the pulling down of strong holds; Casting down imaginations [internal], and every high thing that exalteth itself against the knowledge of God, and bringing into captivity every thought [internal] to the obedience of Christ; And having in a readiness to revenge all disobedience [external], when your obedience is fulfilled (2Corinthians 10:4-6).*

Every territory should be keenly aware of our unwavering stance regarding the Kingdom in the earth. Scripture declares that the Kingdom suffers violence, but the violent take it (non-submissive territories) by force. We heal the sick, raise the dead and cast out devils declaring the Kingdom of God has come!

This book explores ten principles gleaned from David's victory over Goliath. The purpose is to help you align yourself with the

Eternal Purpose of God, as well as your specific sub-purpose. Remember, your purpose must be encased in the Eternal Purpose of God, which is to reclaim every thing stolen by satan. This book will help you to identify your calling. It will teach you how to develop the gift God has entrusted to you for His purpose. Finally, I believe the Holy Spirit will use this book to help you know exactly where your ministry is expressed. God wants you to know His will for your life.

Rethinking The Gifts

The Acts and Gifts of the Holy Ghost

The gifts distributed by the Holy Spirit as well as the ascension or five-fold ministry gifts given by Jesus Christ play a significant role in the lives of believers. In this chapter you will learn how the Godhead synchronistically orchestrates the gifts in the earth. You will also leave this chapter with what I believe to be an accurate view of the ascension gifts[3].

> It is important, brethren, that you should have clear knowledge on the subject of spiritual gifts (1Corinthians 12:1 Weymouth New Testament)

Paul outlines a list of spirit gifts in his letter to the Corinthian church, and concludes with an admonition to 'covet the best gifts'

---

[3] The terms five-fold ministry and ascension gifts are used interchangeably in this book.

(1Corinthians 12:31). Unfortunately this little phrase has led too many to gravitate to the so-called power gifts to be self-proclaimed experts in prophecy, healing and miracle working. There is a performance-based mentality driving much of the ministry exhibited in churches. Validation, anointing and self-worth are measured by what you can do, rather than who you are to serve.

Spiritual gifts are not toys. They are not intended to be wielded by immature believers looking to impress others. Spiritual gifts are special endowments given by the Holy Spirit to strengthen the Body of Christ. The only time they are to be used is to build up and strengthen believers. They are never to become a platform for personal gain and notoriety.

But let your desires be turned to the more important things given by the Spirit. And now I am pointing out to you an even better way. (1Corinthians 12:31 Bible in Basic English)

Much of the teaching surrounding spiritual gifts are drawn from the twelfth chapter of first Corinthians. The nine gifts have been categorized, analyzed, dissected and discussed in an attempt to show what they are and how they work. Yet, Paul makes a transitional statement that alerts us to the foundation of all gifts. He points to a better way. This better way is not focused on the *activity* of the gift, but rather the *attitude* you need before using it.

Chapter thirteen of first Corinthians is often called the love chapter. It is read at weddings, Valentine's Day events, and special programs where love is the theme. Because it is often read as a 'stand alone' chapter, we have failed to understand that chapter thirteen is a continuation of Paul's discussion of spiritual gifts. Thus, chapters twelve, thirteen and fourteen of first Corinthians all have the same primary subject.

Why is this important?

I want you to settle it in your spirit now that whatever gift the Holy Spirit entrusts to you, is for building the Body of Christ. If you have any ulterior motive to be known, recognized or heralded as an apostle, prophet, healer, miracle worker or the like, you may need to reassess your desire to know your calling, purpose or ministry.

Ministry and spiritual gifts are not about you. Can God commission you as an apostle? Yes, it is possible. Can you be a prophet? Yes, if God so wills. Can you be used to heal the sick? Absolutely, and I pray you will. Yet, if you violate the integrity of scripture, live a questionable lifestyle and use spiritual or ministry gifts to promote yourself, then you have misunderstood everything Paul taught about gifts.

THE ACTIVE POWER OF THE GODHEAD

In the beginning when God said let *us* make man in our image, it established from the onset that the Godhead, consisting of the Father, Son and Holy Spirit, would play an active role in the activity of man in the earth (Genesis 1:26). Beyond God using the plurality of '*us*', the very word from which God is translated is *Elohiym*, which describes the plurality of the Supreme God. Paul's letter to the Corinthians reveals the Godhead at work in us both collectively and individually.

Now there are diversities of gifts, <u>but the same Spirit</u> (1Corithians 12:4)

There are many gifts in the Body of Christ. Paul prefaces this letter with the concern he had with the idolization of spiritual gifts exhibited by the Corinthians (1Corinthians 12:1-2). These gifts are distributed by the Holy Spirit.

There is a close parallel between the Corinthian Church and many of the churches today. There is an inordinate preoccupation with gifts in the church that falsely elevates one ministry over another. The improper understanding of the gifts has fed into the hierarchal mindset that is never found in scriptures.

Apostles have replaced Constantinian style Bishops with networks of churches under them. Modern day apostles have become the very opposite of the apostles portrayed in scripture. Apostleship has become a prestigious position rather than a foundational role with prophets in the church.

Prophets have evolved into a mysterious group who spew out a plethora of spiritual edicts. Most prophecies are in the blessing category, followed closely by prophesying spiritual gifts. Those prophets who prophesy the so-called 'hard words' are often considered 'deep', and they often take pride in becoming social and religious martyrs because of their offensive approach to ministry. Very few prophets speak from the ultimate purposes of God, thus their predictions are often shortsighted and fail to move believers toward divine conclusions.

Here are the facts. The earth is filled with apostles – both genuine and false. There a thousands of prophets – again both genuine and false. There are hundreds of thousands of spiritual teachers, miracle workers, pastors, evangelists, and people with the gifts of hospitality, giving, mercy and so on. Each of these gifts was given by the Holy Spirit for the benefit of all believers (1Corinthians 12:7). One gift is not greater than another (1Corinthians 12:11-18). Wherever the spirit deposits a gift, it is for the health of the whole body, not the elevation of the one entrusted with it.

And there are differences of administrations, but the same Lord....
(1Corinthians 12:5)

Man was created to function in the earth. This is a foundational truth you need to understand how ministry coexists with purpose. You cannot assume that your gift is for everyone. Whatever the Holy Spirit has entrusted to you is to be used only where the Lord decides. Once a gift has been given by the Holy Spirit, the Lord Himself administers its use in the earth.

I am an apostle – but I am not an apostle to everybody (1Corinthians 9:2). In October of 2008 the Lord told me that He had called me to the culture and atmosphere of the region I live. I have been assigned a ministry by Jesus Christ that will only function accurately where Jesus has assigned me. Although I may travel around the world, my calling is specifically given to me for the region I live. If I become intimidated by or jealous of another apostles' work, it is proof that I do not know my own assignment. Many others have the same gift that I have, but what differentiates us is the assignment we have been given by the Lord. Problems arise when we assume we are called to everybody.

> For we dare not make ourselves of the number, or compare ourselves with some that commend themselves: <u>but they measuring themselves by themselves, and comparing themselves among themselves, are not wise.</u> But we will not boast of things without our measure, but according to the measure of the rule which God hath distributed to us, a measure to reach even unto you. <u>For we stretch not ourselves beyond our measure,</u> as though we reached not unto you: for we are come as far as to you also in preaching the gospel of Christ: Not boasting of things without our measure, that is, of other men's labours; but having hope, <u>when your faith is increased, that we shall be enlarged by you according to our rule abundantly, To preach the gospel in the regions beyond you,</u> and not to boast in another man's line of things made ready to our hand. (2Corinthians 10:12-15)

...all that David did for God's purpose in his generation is directly connected to whatever you are assigned to do in this generation.

Paul recognized the boundaries of his ministry. He refused to boast or stretch himself beyond his assignment.

He exposed the ignorance of making comparison among others. He did not build his work on what had been done by other apostles. Paul thoroughly understood that when he was successful in the work God had given him, that the potential for him to expand into other regions was much greater. Your success or failure is rooted in your willingness to understand and stay within the boundaries established for you by the Lord. Allow the Lord Jesus Christ to administer your gift.

And there are diversities of operations, <u>but it is the same God</u> which worketh all in all (1Corinthians 12:6)

This is the heart of purpose. It is God who wisely orchestrates individual and corporate callings, individual and corporate purposes, and individual and corporate ministries into pathways that will produce His ultimate purpose in the earth. If I fail to see how my purpose is connected to yours proves that I am blinded to God's universal purpose. Even if one of us is in error, God's wisdom can bring alignment and direction towards His universal end (Romans 8:28).

All activity must be deliberately aligned with Eternal Purpose. Our individual purpose must be accurately synchronized with God's ultimate purpose. Our individual purpose must never be measured in terms of size, greatness, or popularity. The only measurement we have is whether our purpose is accurately connected to God's Eternal Purpose.

For David, after having been useful to his own generation in accordance with God's purpose, did fall asleep... (Acts 13:36 Weymouth's New Testament)[4]

David is dead. He lived and walked this earth over three thousand years ago. Yet, scripture declares that he was useful to his own generation in accordance with God's divine purpose. The activities in David's life (good and bad) all found alignment in God's ultimate purpose. You live in a generation far removed from the time of David. Yet, all that David did for God's purpose in his generation is directly connected to whatever you are assigned to do in this generation.

In whom the god of this world hath blinded the minds of them which believe not, lest the light of the glorious gospel of Christ, who is the image of God, should shine unto them (2Corinthians 4:4).

And the disciples came, and said unto him, Why speakest thou unto them in parables? He answered and said unto them, Because it is given unto you to know the mysteries of the kingdom of heaven, but to them it is not given. For whosoever hath, to him shall be given, and he shall have more abundance: but whosoever hath not, from him shall be taken away even that he hath. Therefore speak I to them in parables: because they seeing see not; and hearing they hear not, neither do they understand. And in them is fulfilled the prophecy of Esaias, which saith, By hearing ye shall

---

[4] Harper and Row Publishers, Inc. and James Clarke and Company LTD. *Weymouth's New Testament in Modern Speech* by Richard Francis Weymouth.

hear, and shall not understand; and seeing ye shall see, and shall not perceive: <u>For this people's heart is waxed gross, and their ears are dull of hearing, and their eyes they have closed; lest at any time they should see with their eyes, and hear with their ears, and should understand with their heart, and should be converted, and I should heal them.</u> But blessed are your eyes, for they see: and your ears, for they hear. For verily I say unto you, That many prophets and righteous men have desired to see those things which ye see, and have not seen them; and to hear those things which ye hear, and have not heard them. (Matthew 13:10-17)

Paul described a blindness that is perpetrated upon the mind of unbelievers by *the god of this world*. The word *world* in second Corinthians 4:4 is translated from the Greek word *aion*. It describes an age or specific time period. Some translations accurately *say the god of this age*.

I submit that the same *god of this world*, the god of this age and time we live, is still working to blind the minds of *unbelievers* to keep them from accurately seeing the glorious gospel, and is also working to blind *believers* from seeing God's Eternal Purpose. The god of this world or age seeks to distort our view of God's purposes in the age we live. Inaccurate sight produces inaccurate action (Matthew 13:14; John 12:40). If you fail to see God's purposes, your actions will be tainted by the influences of your current season and environment.

Religious thinking has been used by satan to redirect the focus of the church. First, the eyes of the church are too often on each other. By focusing on denominational pit wars, the church is continually being torn apart by religious separatism.

Second, the eyes of the church have been distracted by world systems. The extreme on one side is there are those who reject the 'world' and consider themselves spiritual martyrs by assuming that their dress codes, isolated lifestyles and religious rules will keep them tainted from the sinful world. The extreme on the other side is that the eyes of the church have been blinded by the lure of world glamour. These churches boast themselves in bigness, luxury, extravagance, and measure what they consider success by the world's standards. Both sides are grossly in error.

Jesus said we are *in the world*, but not *of the world* (John 17:9-16). Paul admonished us not to be conformed to the world, but rather to be transformed by renewed thought processes (Romans 12:2). Jesus taught us to pray that the Kingdom of God would be established on earth, as it is in heaven (Matthew 6:10). The emphasis of most Christians is to get to heaven rather than establishing the Kingdom of God in the earth. Thus, the church is blind to their true purpose. The domino effect of this incorrect sight effects ministry and spiritual gifts. If you don't know His Eternal purpose, it will be difficult to accurately know how ministry or spiritual gifts function.

Jesus purposely taught in parables. Parables exposes where people are in their relationship to God. He taught so only a select group would comprehend what He was saying. This is crucial for us to understand. He described a people whose ears were dull of hearing, which means they could not accurately discern the voice of God. Also, they had of their own volition closed their eyes. In other words they refused to see what God was doing. If they had accurately heard and seen, then Jesus would have been able to convert and heal them.

The Greek word translated as *converted* is *epistrepho*. It means to turn from one thing and turn to another. Accurate sight and accurate hearing demands that we turn away from incorrectness and turn toward alignment with the Father, in His Son Jesus Christ. It is in the turning that healing flows. We turn by confessing that we are moving in the wrong direction. Then our faithful and just Lord will forgive us for missing the mark (sin), and cleanse us (heal) from the effects of our error. As long as our ears are dull and we close our eyes, we will continue to walk outside of the purposes of God.

To seek your calling, or to try and understand your purpose or attempt to pursue a ministry outside of God's eternal purpose only serves to perpetuate the dysfunction already active in the church. It is critical that going forward, you think of spiritual and ministry gifts and their relationship to God's purposes.

Hierarchy
The End of Religious Thinking

Over the past thirty or so years, there has been a progressive acceptance of the five-fold ministry gifts – specifically the prophet and apostle. Unfortunately, the structure of the church that came into existence around the fourth century has dictated our understanding of how ministry gifts function in the contemporary church.

In this chapter, hierarchy will be discussed because the five-fold gifts have succumbed into a top-down system of overseeing local churches. Apostles are at the top of this religious pecking order, followed by the prophet. Evangelists, pastors and teachers too often either disappear, or become a merged gift subordinate to the apostle or prophet. One may become an apostle-teacher, prophet-pastor or a prophetic apostle who pastors a local church.

Apostles in particular have become modern day 'bishops' who oversee networks of churches. Some take pride in having hundreds of churches 'under' them. However, when you study all the apostles in the New Testament, not one had such a network. They had solid relationships with several churches, but those churches were independent and autonomous governed by local elders. In other words, the first century apostles were adept in *networking*, but did not manage or oversee *networks* of churches.

Before we delve into God's process, you need to understand the issue of hierarchy. It is a subtle and silent enemy of the Kingdom of God. When I first wrote this book, hierarchy was hardly ever discussed in the church. Yet, scripture clearly shows us that the top down structure of most church systems was never in the mind of the Father.

We are Kingdom citizens. Hierarchy is a foreign concept in the Kingdom of God. World governments are hierarchal. Businesses are hierarchal. Most churches are hierarchal. It is not something we think about, it is just the way it is. The *'who reports to who'* or *'who is submitted to who'* mindset has unfortunately created an atmosphere wherein people clamor for position rather than service.

This book is written to help you identify your specific calling, purpose and ministry. This chapter has been added to this book to set the principles of calling, purpose and ministry in their proper context.

To be clear, no calling, purpose or ministry can function accurately in the earth if they are hierarchal in nature. Without putting them into context you will run the risk of succumbing to the hierarchal mindset that rules the world and has stymied the church for so long.

The Merriam-Webster's Collegiate Dictionary defines hierarchy in religious terms. Specifically it first defines hierarchy as a division of angels. I believe this relates to our understanding of Cherubim, Seraphim and Archangels (Genesis 3:24; Isaiah 6:2; Jude 1:9).

Hierarchy in the church is a governing system wherein individuals hold a place of authority over others primarily by reason of their title or position. Those under submission are told to respect the office and individuals who hold it. The problem is that at times the individual holding the office is either under qualified or not qualified at all.

Some years ago I ministered at a gathering in Chicago wherein I gave the following analogy regarding those in various ministry offices:

> Imagine going to your local grocery looking for a can of pork and beans. When you arrive, every can in the store is unmarked. Every can looks identical to the other cans throughout the store. In the midst of this, you find one can that is clearly labeled 'pork and beans'. You purchase that can, and go home expecting to find in the can what the label indicates on the outside. In essence, you put a demand on the contents of the can in hopes of finding pork and beans inside.

Too often in ministry, we are surrounded by those who claim to be apostles, prophets, evangelists and the like. We go to them and put a demand on the office they claim to hold, but too often we find we are expecting too much from empty containers. When they fail to produce the leadership we anticipated, we are told to submit to them because after all, they are called and God's anointed ones.

> ...there is an accepted hierarchal paradigm in the church that is normative and systemic for many believers

When I shared this story, I was showing how some people hold 'spiritual offices' that they are not qualified to have. But this also exposes the danger of hierarchy – an unqualified, unprepared individual can be in a position of perceived authority based on a title alone. This is a picture of dysfunctional hierarchy. That is, a person occupying a spiritual office they are unqualified to hold, and demanding submission from others based on that office.

Then Samuel took the horn of oil, and anointed him in the midst of his brethren: and the Spirit of the LORD came upon David from that day forward. So Samuel rose up, and went to Ramah. But the Spirit of the LORD departed from Saul, and an evil spirit from the LORD troubled him (1Samuel 16:13-14).

The Lord placed His Spirit upon David and immediately withdrew it from Saul. Yet, Saul still held the office of king. It was over a decade later that David became the king. Like Saul, there are some who do not have the grace or anointing to hold the office they occupy. They suppress and try to destroy those who they consider a threat. On more than one occasion, Saul tried to kill David. My personal opinion is that Saul saw in David the anointing he formally had. It is the same phenomenon that took place when satan was expelled from heaven. The devil hates us because our praise replaces the glory he once held around the Throne of God.

On the other hand, there is an accepted hierarchal paradigm in the church that is normative and systemic for many believers. We submit to leaders who we believe have our best interest in their hearts. They are the professional clergy 'called of God' to lead the laity – or at least that's what we have always assumed. Each side – clergy and laity – passively take for granted their roles in the church, and as long as each side stays within the perceived boundaries of their status, the church is at peace.

In many churches, the 'clergy' have been trained in Bible Schools, Christian colleges and Seminaries. There is nothing wrong with this high-level training and it should be encouraged. However, implicit in this training is that they are uniquely qualified to lead the so-called laity on their spiritual journeys. They teach, they counsel, they visit, they pray and do all the spiritual things we believe clergy should do. But here is the caveat – there is no biblical basis for the clergy/laity division. Let that sink in for a moment. The concept of clergy over laity is not a part of the Lord's church.

THE ERRONEOUS CONCEPT OF CLERGY AND LAITY

The very concept of 'clergy/laity' invokes a religious upper and lower class in the Body of Christ, when in fact there is no scriptural basis for such a distinction.

Historically, the distinction between clergy and laity took root in the fourth century when the structure of the church was drastically compromised. During this time the church embraced a secular model of an upper and lower caste.

In the Greco-Roman world, *kleros* referred to municipal administrators and *laos* referred to those who were ruled by them. In the church, *kleros* became associated with those who were sacred, while *laos* described a lower secular class of people. This distinction became so pervasive that by the twelfth century *kleros* were nearly always associated with those who were saints and *laos* were those who compromised Christianity.[5]

Some biblical scholars believe the error of hierarchy began in the first century. In the book of Revelation, there are two significant statements regarding the Nicolaitans. Both referred to things that the Lord hates. First, He hates the *deeds* of the Nicolaitans which He commended the Church in Ephesus for hating too. Second, He hates the *doctrine* of the Nicolaitans and warned them about tolerating those among them that taught it.

---

[5] For an excellent study of clergy/laity read Greg Ogden's UNFINISHED BUSINESS *Returning the ministry to the people of God* © 1990 Zondervan

*Remember therefore from whence thou art fallen, and repent, and do the
first works; or else I will come unto thee quickly, and will remove thy
candlestick out of his place, except thou repent. But this thou hast, that
thou hatest the deeds of the Nicolaitans, which I also hate. He that hath
an ear, let him hear what the Spirit saith unto the churches; To him that
overcometh will I give to eat of the tree of life, which is in the midst of the
paradise of God. (Revelation 2:5-7)*

*So hast thou also them that hold the doctrine of the Nicolaitans, which
thing I hate. (Revelation 2:15)*

Some believe that the Nicolaitans were a sect that emanated from
Nicolas, one of the seven men selected to care for the Grecian widows
(Acts 6:5). John Wesley wrote:

> That thou hatest the works of the Nicolaitans-Probably so
> called from Nicolas, one of the seven deacons, Acts 6:5. Their
> doctrines and lives were equally corrupt. They allowed the
> most abominable lewdness and adulteries, as well as sacrificing
> to idols; all which they placed among things indifferent, and
> pleaded for as branches of Christian liberty.

Dr. Victor Choudrie, in his book GREET THE EKKLESIA! *The Church
In Your House*[6] wrote:

---

[6] Greet the Ekkesia: The Church In Your House © 1997 – 2006 (nine editions) Dr.
Victor Choudrie pg 26 & 89

Jesus Hates A Hierarchal Church: Nicolas, supposedly one of the seven deacons chosen along with Stephen, went to the Ekklesias and wrecked them by dividing them into "speaking brothers" and "listening brothers." "Nicos" means "conquering" and "laos" means "ordinary people" hence; "Nicolaitan" came to mean "conquering the laity." Jesus hates this clerical hierarchy because it drives a wedge between the religious elite and the ordinary believer (Rev. 2:6 1Pet. 5:2,3).

Nelson's Illustrated Bible Dictionary clearly ties Nicolas with the Nicolaitans. It states that the church fathers accused Nicolas of denying the true Christian faith and founding the heretical sect known as the Nicolaitans.[7] Whereas scholars do not fully agree on whether the Nicolaitans were a sect derived from Nicolas, however there is universal agreement on the meaning of his name – *victorious over the people; Nicolaus, a heretic.*[8]

The text in Revelation speaks to both the deeds and the doctrines of the Nicolaitans. Doctrines precede deeds. In other words, you normally do (*deeds*) what you believe (*doctrine*). The contemporary church has embraced the clergy/laity division. Our structure and methodologies (*deeds*) reflect what we believe regarding clergy and laity (*doctrine*). If Dr. Choudrie is correct in his assertion of *teaching brothers* versus *listening brothers*, then it is the error of the Nicolaitans

---

[7] See Nicolas, Nelson's Illustrated Bible Dictionary © 1986 Thomas Nelson Publishers

[8] See Nicolas, Strong's Exhaustive Concordance of the Bible

that was the root of their licentious deeds. They were obviously taught wrong by the teaching brothers, and their actions reflected that error.

Today, we honestly and innocently believe that there is a clergy class, the spiritual specialists who lead and guide us, and a laity class who must be led and implicitly do not carry the spiritual proficiency of the clergy. Throughout this book, I will examine how this erroneous view of ministry can have a negative effect on your calling, purpose and ministry.

THE TEN PRINCIPLES

There are ten principles gleaned from David's encounter with Goliath that help us discover our calling, purpose and ministry.

Principle 1:   Wait for God's season

Principle 2:   You are not indispensable

Principle 3:   Guard your heart

Principle 4:   Be responsible

Principle 5:   Be aware of your surroundings

Principle 6:   Beware of distractions

Principle 7:   Don't lose your enthusiasm

Principle 8:   Use your gifts and talents

Principle 9:   Commit to overcome all obstacles

Principle 10: Keep your eyes on the goal

Before we delve into these principles, it is important that you understand the atmosphere required for them to function accurately. As I have discussed the danger of hierarchal structures, I must also introduce you to the antithesis of hierarchy which is permissional.

Permissional
The Culture of the Church

When this book was first written, I had in my spirit a directive from the Lord to, *"Provide a viable outlet for the ministry gifts."* My thinking at that time was to show individuals how to find their particular spiritual niche in life (i.e. their calling). Unfortunately, I had not accurately connected the dots to see how calling, purpose and ministry functioned in the church. My focus was on the individual rather than the Body of Christ. If your calling, purpose and ministry are not for the benefit of the Body of Christ, then it runs the risk of being self-serving and dysfunctional.

Since 2001, the Holy Spirit has taken me on a fascinating journey that has revealed how the first century church functioned and how it applies to us in the twenty-first century. This has prompted the need to update this book to reflect the values and structure of the first century church.

> *And he gave some, apostles; and some, prophets; and some, evangelists; and some, pastors and teachers; <u>For the perfecting of the saints, for the work of the ministry,</u> for the edifying of the body of Christ: (Ephesians 4:11-12)*

Underlying this edition is that we are now in the season referred to by some as *'the day of the saints'* or the 'saints movement'. This is the season where the Holy Spirit is bringing emphasis to the 'work of ministry' being done by the saints. As in times past, the church as we know it is trying to create the work of ministry in a structure that is foreign to what existed when Paul penned these words in his letter to the church in Ephesus (Ephesians 4:11-16). During that time, there were no church systems like we see today. Believers did not *'go to church'*. They understood that they 'were the church'. They gathered from house-to-house breaking bread, edifying, exhorting and strengthening one another (Acts 2:46).

In the first century, the church was led by a plurality of elders rather than a lone pastor (Acts 20:17; Titus 1:5). There were no 'programs and events', but rather a body of believers committed to the purposes of the Father in heaven. Therefore, any biblical reference to calling, purpose and ministry must be understood in this context (Romans 8:28; Ephesians 4:1; 2Timothy 1:9).

Today, most equate the church to a building rather than the people who occupy it. These buildings are designed similarly to a lecture hall. People file into these structures to be spiritually 'entertained' by praise teams, dance ministries and dynamic preachers. The auditorium style setting both implicitly and explicitly says that ministry is limited to those on the platform. Those sitting in the pews or chairs generally understand they are to be listeners and financial supporters. Their participation is limited to clapping their hands to the music, saying "amen" to the preacher, a responsive reading and if they are really blessed, they may be called up to receive a personal prophecy.

If you are among those who believe you have a calling on your life, you generally understand that your opportunity is limited to one of the few positions available on the platform. In some church systems there are also 'lay-leadership' positions you can pursue. In most cases, to get there, you must go through the process outlined by those in charge. This is not necessarily wrong per se, but it often has the effect of limiting access into ministry. It could take you several years to even be recognized. When you are finally licensed or ordained in your calling, you now find you have very little outlet to express it. Internally, you must wait your turn. External opportunities often only come through self-promotion, and sometimes even those opportunities are regulated by those you 'sit under'. For some, this scenario may seem extreme, but there are many who are experiencing this right now.

Much has been taught about personal calling and ministry. Purpose has often been blurred within the confines of a corporate church vision. Most teaching has been geared towards the individual's calling being used for the good of the church. In other words, whatever you believe you have been called to do must benefit the corporate church vision.

The emphasis has been more on 'performance' and 'position' rather than servanthood. People clamor and politic to become something (an apostle, a prophet, an elder, etc.) because primary validation comes from the corporate church rather than from the Lord. Thus, calling and ministry have become a means to personal gain (2Peter 2:3).

One goal in this book is to establish the understanding of calling, purpose and ministry in the context of the New Testament Church, not the corporate church systems. There is a difference.

The New Testament Church is organic and void of hierarchy, whereas the corporate church is often a top down governmental system that often limits ministry to few. Leadership in the New Testament Church is *supportive* in nature, whereas leadership in the corporate church is *positional* in nature. The focal point of supportive leadership is to undergird believers as they pursue whatever God has called them to. In contrast, the general focal point of positional leadership is to find placement to exercise perceived authority.

Because of our misunderstanding of New Testament Church structure it is often difficult to see how the church leadership is to function. The functional culture of the New Testament Church is *permissional*, whereas the functional culture of the corporate church is *hierarchal*. The New Testament Church flows horizontally on a linear plane, and the corporate church flows vertically from the top down.

In my book, NO LONGER CHURCH AS USUAL I define the church as follows:

> The New Testament Church is an assembly of believers, committed to the Kingdom Mandate, who gather one or more times each week under the Headship of Jesus Christ; who are submitted to each other in love; who support each other's ongoing work of being and making disciples of the Lord Jesus Christ; who edify, exhort and comfort one another; who submit and relate to elders, ministry gifts and apostolic leaders; who participate in planting and supporting new assemblies of believers to do the same with their prayers, time, finances and material resources.

I teach that the church follows five primary values, all of which preceded the many doctrines we see today. Those five values are (1) the Lordship of Jesus Christ (2) the priesthood of every believer (3) the Holy Spirit – His acts and His gifts (4) growth through covenant relationships and (5) no one lacking among us.

The church has a sole mission given to it by the Father at creation, and reiterated by Jesus Christ and the apostles. It is the Kingdom Mandate which is to be fruitful, multiply, replenish and subdue the earth (Genesis 1:28). Understanding the definition of the church, while living the values of the church and simultaneously pursuing the mandate of the church can only be done in a *permissional culture*. It is a culture that reflects the values and structure of the first century church.

WHAT IS A PERMISSIONAL CULTURE?

Every citizen of the Kingdom of God is a king and priest with both ministry and redemptive authority. We exercise our ministry and kingdom authority in the earth – not heaven (Romans 5:17; 2Corinthians 5:18; Revelation 5:10).

> *And ye shall be unto me a kingdom of priests, and an holy nation. These [are] the words which thou shalt speak unto the children of Israel. (Exodus 19:6)*

> *These shall make war with the Lamb, and the Lamb shall overcome them: for he is Lord of lords, and King of kings: and they that are with him [are] called, and chosen, and faithful. (Revelation 17:14)*

> *And he hath on [his] vesture and on his thigh a name written, KING OF KINGS, AND LORD OF LORDS. (Revelation 19:16)*

If you understand that you are a king, you also need to understand how to function as a king. A king does not need the permission of another king to exercise his rule and authority. He is permitted by nature of his office to make whatever decisions he deems necessary for the benefit of his kingdom. Thus, we discover the *permissional* aspect of church government. In essence, the church as a whole is a *permissional society*. You are permitted, by nature of your kingly authority, to pursue your assignment in the earth.

The term *permissional* implies the on-going granting of permission by a higher authority. A *permissional society* recognizes that every citizen has been granted the same permission by the same higher authority. A *permissional society* does not mean that everyone does what they want when they want to. Therefore *permissional* is not to be confused with *permissive*. By no means is a *permissional society* a religious free-for-all. How does a *permissional society* function without chaos?

KINGS AND PRIESTS

You are a king according to scripture, but there is a greater King – Jesus Christ. He is King of kings (1Timothy 6:15; Revelation 17:14; 19:16). Your kingdom and my kingdom must be fully submitted to His Kingdom, otherwise we are anarchist and rebellious.

We must continuously submit our kingdoms to Jesus Christ. This is done by daily confessing His lordship over our lives. The strength of our confession comes from what we believe in our hearts. If I truly believe my confession – that He is Lord – then I am willing to take up my cross daily and follow Him – regardless of my personal cost (Luke 9:23; 14:26-35).

The purpose of His Kingdom must be the purpose of your kingdom and my kingdom. He did not entrust us with a kingdom to function separate from His. Yes, we are expected to be productive with our kingdom, but that productivity is for His glory and not our gain (John 15:16).

How then can His Kingdom have any order when every citizen is a king and permitted to pursue the expansion of his or her kingdom? Such would be impossible if we fail to understand that a permissional society is balanced by obedience and accountability.

Obedience and accountability can only function in an atmosphere of *mutual submission*. I must first commit myself to obey every instruction I receive from the Word of God and the Holy Spirit. My sphere of kingdom rule must be totally submitted to Jesus Christ, and I must also be submitted to you.

The same applies to you. You too must first obey every command of Jesus Christ. You must submit your sphere of kingdom rule under the authority of Jesus Christ, so that it can be a valuable asset to other 'kings' in the Lord's Kingdom. Our only purpose is to insure that Jesus Christ is glorified and His Kingdom is advanced. In the earth, our individual kingdoms must serve to advance the work of other kings in the Lord's Kingdom.

For though I be free from all [men], yet have I made myself servant unto all, that I might gain the more. (1Corinthians 9:19)

For, brethren, ye have been called unto liberty; only <u>use not liberty for an</u> <u>occasion to the flesh, but by love serve one another</u>. (Galatians 5:13)

<u>Submit yourselves to every ordinance</u> of man for the Lord's sake: whether it be to the king, as supreme; Or unto governors, as unto them that are sent by him for the punishment of evildoers, and for the praise of them that do well. For so is the will of God, that with well doing ye may put to silence the ignorance of foolish men: As free, and <u>not using your liberty</u> <u>for a cloke of maliciousness, but as the servants of God</u>. (1Peter 2:13-16)

I am an apostle. I have been entrusted with a realm of authority (or kingdom) by the revelation Jesus Christ has given to me. Your kingdom may differ from mine. The revelation you have from Jesus Christ is accompanied by the authority to advance it. Our individual kingdoms must find a place of mutual submission to each other for the glory of the Lord. If there is a clash between my kingdom and yours, it means that one or both of us are not in obedience or submitted to the King of kings. Conflicts are proof that one or both of us have placed our own kingdom above His. Quarrels imply that we have lost sight of His purpose in the earth.

The permissional society fails when individuals become self-serving. It is diluted when the desire for personal glory takes preeminence over Divine Will. The Holy Spirit works through each of us accomplishing the purposes of God in the earth. If each of us accurately hear and obey the Holy Spirit, there would be no conflicts among us. However, we know that as humans our flesh from time to time will get in the way. So how is this handled?

ACCOUNTABILITY IN THE HOUSE

Believers who try to 'go it alone' will eventually get into trouble. God did not design us or His church to operate in isolation. Permissional does not mean a person has the right to 'do their own thing' outside of interaction with other believers. It is safe to have other believers have the opportunity to pray with them and give advice.

> But exhort one another daily, while it is called To day; lest any of you be hardened through the deceitfulness of sin (Hebrews 3:13)

In Hebrews 3:13, we are instructed to exhort one another daily. Failure to do so could lead to one's heart becoming hardened through the deceitfulness of sin. The Amplified Bible specifically states that daily exhortation helps to keep one from entering into 'settled rebellion'.

The Greek verb translated *exhort* is *parakeleo*. This word is very similar to the Greek noun *parakletos* which is used as an adjective to describe the Holy Spirit as the *comforter*. Both words give the suggestion of one coming along side another person. The *parakeletos* or *comforter* comes along side a person to aid. It also was used for one who pleaded another's cause, an advocate or intercessor. The verb *parakeleo* or *exhort* means to come along side another to urge them to pursue a certain course of conduct, always looking to the future.[9]

---

[9] See comforter and exhort *Vines Expository Dictionary of New Testament Words*

In a permissional society, where a believer is free to pursue their assignment from God, exhortation is an important factor. To have someone 'come along side' a believer and urge them to pursue a certain course of conduct implies a relational closeness that serves to protect them from slipping into error.

CALLING, PURPOSE AND
MINISTRY IN A PERMISSIONAL SOCIETY

In a permissional society, we must never lose sight of the two-fold aspect of our purpose. We must first be fully submitted to the Lord Jesus Christ and His purpose to establish God's Kingdom in the earth. And second, we must always remember that our calling, purpose and ministry are to bring Him glory by being an asset to other believers in their quest to bring God glory through their calling, purpose and ministry.

Whatever my assignment is from God is to be strength to you. Whatever your assignment is from God is to be strength to me. Collectively our assignments help accomplish His purposes and bring Him glory.

Principle 1
Wait For God's Season

GOD WILL EXALT YOU IN DUE SEASON. HE WILL EXPOSE YOUR DESTINY TO THOSE WHO DON'T BELIEVE YOU HAVE ONE!

And let us not be weary in well doing: for in due season we shall reap, if we faint not. (Galatians 6:9)

In your heart you know that God has a purpose for your life. You've tried sharing it with a few friends and acquaintances. No one appears to believe you. So you continue ushering, knowing that you are a prophet. You are hidden in the back row of the choir, yearning for the opportunity to preach. You drudge daily in a dead end job, with visions of a great business in your spirit. You believe you are anointed to teach, but you can't raise the funds for further education. You are frustrated because your clear call from God is locked up and hidden behind circumstance and situations.

David was assigned to keep his father's sheep. Little is said about his older brothers, but it is clear when the Prophet Samuel showed up to anoint a king, David wasn't in the house.

And the LORD said unto Samuel, How long wilt thou mourn for Saul, seeing I have rejected him from reigning over Israel? fill thine horn with oil, and go, I will send thee to Jesse the Bethlehemite: for I have provided me a king among his sons. (1Samuel 16:1)

Imagine how proud Jesse was to have a famous prophet show up to anoint one of his sons to potentially be the next king of Israel. I am sure that he schooled his boys on the proper decorum. Each one knew exactly what to say and how to act.

Again, Jesse made seven of his sons to pass before Samuel. And Samuel said unto Jesse, The LORD hath not chosen these. And Samuel said unto Jesse, Are here all thy children? And he said, There remaineth yet the youngest, and, behold, he keepeth the sheep. And Samuel said unto Jesse, Send and fetch him: for we will not sit down till he come hither. (1Samuel 16:10-11)

Notice that the above passage began with the word 'again'. Samuel most likely inspected and re-inspected each of Jesse's older boys several times. One by one, Samuel examined each of them. One by one he had to reject them at the Word of the Lord. He was possibly beginning to question if he had heard properly from the Lord. While the older brothers were being considered for kingship, David was keeping the sheep. He hadn't been prepared to meet the prophet. In fact, if Samuel had not asked if there were more brothers, he would possibly have never known that David existed. It was only at Samuel's inquiry that David was invited into the house.

David was a stark contrast to his brothers. Rather than being well dressed, he wore his shepherd's garments. Instead of being clean and well groomed, he carried the odor of sheep. He did not look like the future king of Israel. David's father, Jesse, nor his brothers, had considered David a candidate for kingship.

There are times when you feel surrounded by those who don't see your potential. Your current position in life keeps you hidden. You see others around you being considered for promotion. Their visibility and stature seemed to make them the obvious choice for advancement. As they move ahead, you remain in the field with someone else's sheep. It is in times like these that you should know that God has provided a 'Samuel' for you.

Somewhere in this world is that special person that God has prepared to connect you to your destiny. This person may not come from among your friends and relatives. This person may not be a member of your local church. It may not be a person at all. It could possibly be a divinely appointed circumstance or situation. You can rest assured that God's calling is always accompanied by a path to its manifestation. Why then do so many miss God's calling, purpose and ministry for their life? I believe there are four reasons.

REASON NUMBER ONE:
THE SPIRIT OF COMPLAINING

Imagine what would have happened if David had complained about being in the field while his brothers were being considered for promotion? His complaints would have been seasoned with jealousy and bitterness. His attitude towards his father and brothers would have been so negative that Samuel would have rejected him, too. Remember, God looks at the heart (1Samuel 16:7).

Many never move beyond their current circumstances for this very reason. Instead of recognizing their current state as a season of preparation, they complain and murmur. By the time they are considered for any level of promotion, they are so embittered that they become ineffective. Instead of serving in excellence where they are, they work in anxiety, trying to prove their worth. When they fail, because of their own attitude, they make themselves martyrs by blaming others for '*not recognizing their anointing*'.

REASON NUMBER TWO: ANXIETY AND ANGER

The bible teaches us to be careful for nothing (Philippians 4:6). The *American Standard Version* says, 'In nothing be anxious'. The *Conybeare Translation* says, 'Let no care trouble you'. *The Berkley Translation* says, 'Entertain no worry'. And the *Centenary Translation* admonishes us by saying, 'Do not worry about anything'.

Worry is closely linked to anxiety. I believe that some of our theology has created unnecessary worry among those seeking ministry. There is the subtle feeling that there is not enough time to get things done. Consequently, we take shortcuts that sabotage God's plan for our lives.

Another source of anxiety and anger is found in desiring ministry that you may not be called to do. Our view of ministry has been tainted by our perception of what it really is. The image of success has become the 'anointed one' who affects the lives of others. The Lord is seeking those who minister to Him (Ezekiel 44:15). People may benefit from your ministry to the Lord, but your focus should always be to please Him and not individuals.

David's brothers were being considered for kingship. That would seem to be a lofty goal for anyone. However, there could only be one king. Each of his brothers lined up before the prophet for their chance to fame. None of them were 'called' for kingship, but they all tried to position themselves for the role.

I have received numerous calls from individuals seeking my advice as to 'when' they should step out into ministry. Usually, their request is accompanied by an explanation that their current setting is hindering their growth. In some of these cases, they didn't want my advice. They wanted me to verbally cosign their desire to leave a particular ministry.

Scripture declares that 'our gift will make room for us and bring us before great men' (Proverbs 18:16). Implicit is that our talents, skills and or calling will open doors for us. A closer look at this scripture reveals something deeper.

The word gift in Proverbs 18:16 is translated from the Hebrew word *mattan*. Most bibles translate this as gift, but it is interesting to note that The Living Bible: Paraphrased[10] uses the word *bribe* instead of gift. Over the years I have watched many individuals politic and connive for positions. Like Simon the sorcerer, they manipulate situations to make people believe they are some 'great one' (Acts 5:36; 8:9). They use or misuse, spiritual gifts, talents and personal skills to draw attention to themselves. They create an image of themselves designed to draw the attention of man. As long as they get the praises of men they feel important.

WHERE ARE YOU?

The timing to begin your ministry work is solely in the hand of the Lord. Ministry must be nurtured.

Some reading this book serve in a traditionally structured church. Others may be in what I believe is a New Testament structured church where you gather in homes. God knows where you are. His call on your life begins where you are. Things however, don't always go as planned. Unfortunately you run the risk of being hurt or disappointed.

---

[10] *Living Letters* by Kenneth N. Taylor © 1962 by Tyndale House Publishers; *Living Gospels* by Kenneth N. Taylor © 1966 by Tyndale House Publishers; *Living Prophecies* by Kenneth N. Taylor © 1966 by Tyndale House Publishers

This has caused some to run from church to church seeking the best place to manifest their perceived ministry.

Never allow hurt and disappointment to make you run. Things may happen that may discourage you. People may say things that will hurt you. Leaders will at times disappoint you. None of these should ever be the reason to run. It is sad to see how many people take off the moment their feelings are hurt. Leaving is a sign of weakness and immaturity. Children run away from home because they can't get their way. It's the "If I can't get my way, I'll take my little anointing elsewhere".

I was saved February 13, 1974. I immediately connected with a vibrant church, and soon became active as a musician playing for the youth choir. I remained at that wonderful church over fifteen years. Over that time I experienced some hurts, disappointments and some very embarrassing moments. None of them caused me to run away.

In 1987, I was licensed as a minister in that church. It was soon after this that the Lord spoke to me about starting a church[11]. I did not take off, but rather took my belief to my pastor. I gave him a one-year letter of resignation, with the stipulation that if I was wrong I would remain active there. During that year I fulfilled every obligation I had. At the end of the year, I did not have clear direction from the Lord, so I remained in place serving another full year, and was instrumental in helping to develop their children church ministry. When I left, I did so

---

[11] There is much more to this wonderful story, but I have chosen to abbreviate it for this book.

with the blessings of my pastor. Today, I still revere him as my father in ministry.

I then connected with a new church in our area. I began to serve wherever I was needed. I was later appointed as assistant to the Pastor. Again, simply because I served among people, there were times of hurt and disappointment. I don't bring this up to make either church seem bad, but rather to emphasize that although people may create issues for you, it is not an excuse to go running. When the Lord made it clear that it was time to start our church, I gave my pastor at that time a six month written notice. I left in peace and still have a good relationship with that church.

Are there legitimate times to leave when you are hurt or disappointed? Yes. I believe when hurt or disappointment emanates from clear violation of scripture by senior leadership, you may need to leave. You are not required to submit to leadership that commits sexual, moral or financial sin and remain unrepentant.

If you have been hurt, and you honestly believe the Lord is leading you to leave where you are, then do so. However, once you are in a new church, do not immediately try and start a ministry. Submit yourself to your new leadership. Allow time to heal the wounds you may have suffered. Above all, allow the Holy Spirit to correct any error in you.

My point is that you will destroy the path to your destiny by responding incorrectly to hurts and disappointments. Think about Joseph and how he was treated by his brothers, Potiphar, and his fellow prisoners, yet the bible shows us that he maintained his integrity throughout all he endured and maintained the Lord's favor.

Remember how David was persecuted by Saul, yet he maintained an excellent spirit. Think about how Paul suffered at the hands of religious leaders, but he never gave up the fight. Remember that if God has called you, He will make provisions and clear timing to begin your work. Any hurts, persecution or heartache you endure will activate God's Kingdom provision in your behalf (Matthew 5:10).

Anxiety will destroy you. I have encountered those who were very anxious to start a ministry work. Whereas I applaud their desire to obey God, I had to question their motives. I have seen those who have started churches because they felt their current church setting was holding them back. I have seen people leave one church because another church opened the door for them to do their ministry. The most extreme case I've witnessed is an individual who was offered a ministry opportunity in a church after they were removed from ministry in their current church because of an adulterous affair.

If you know people who are disgruntled in their current church, give them time, and they will be disgruntled in yours. Never build a ministry on those who complain about their current church. Never entice people to join you by capitalizing on the faults of other ministries.

If you have friends and relatives who are unsaved and unchurched the answer is simple; minister to them. *Lead them to the Lord Jesus Christ.* Help them to get connected with a church. Don't make yourself their god by assuming they need you to be saved. As for buildings, I have come to realize that brick and mortar buildings are simply tools. Buildings are good to hold people. But you must build people before you ever build buildings.

The above advice is primarily aimed at those who may consider starting a church, but the principles can be used to start any ministry endeavor. You may be called to Youth ministry, jail and prison ministry, evangelism, prophetic or any of a multitude of possibilities. You are called to glorify God and to expand His Kingdom. In a permissional atmosphere the possibilities are endless. Therefore it is imperative that you begin with the right spirit and motives.

> But *when the fulness of the time was come,* God sent forth his Son, made of a woman, made under the law, (Galatians 4:4)

Think about the timing of Jesus' birth. The bible makes it clear that Jesus was born to save us from our sins (John 1:29). In fact, the bible also clearly states that Jesus is the only Name given under heaven and earth by which we can be saved (Acts 4:12). The above passage from Galatians makes it clear that God did not rush Jesus into the earth.

Some historians say that there were approximately four thousand years of biblical history prior to Jesus' birth. In that time, people lived and died. It wasn't until the *fullness of time - when all things were ready,* that God sent Jesus Christ. He wasn't moved by the fact that literally millions would live and die without Him, before He was ever born.[12] God clearly made provisions for them all. Wait on the Lord, and in due season He will establish your work (Psalms 27:14). Don't rush.

The other side of the anxiety coin is those who wait too long. They know God has called them, but they are waiting for the exact and perfect circumstances to launch out. I hate to disappoint you, but the timing of the Lord is not contingent upon circumstances.

And Jesus, walking by the sea of Galilee, saw two brethren, Simon called Peter, and Andrew his brother, casting a net into the sea: for they were fishers. And he saith unto them, Follow me, and I will make you fishers of men. AND THEY STRAIGHTWAY LEFT their nets, and followed him. And going on from thence, he saw other two brethren, James the son of Zebedee, and John his brother, in a ship with Zebedee their father, mending their nets; and he called them. And THEY IMMEDIATELY LEFT the ship and their father, and followed him. (Matthew 4:18-22)

When Peter and Andrew were summoned by Jesus, the bible says that *straightway* they left their nets and followed Him. Likewise, when Jesus called James and John, these brothers *immediately* left their ship. How many do you know would have the courage to response so quickly?

---

[12] God made provisions through the Abrahamic Covenant for those who lived and died prior to the birth of Jesus Christ. His promises to them were fulfilled in Jesus Christ when He led 'captivity captive'(Ephesians 4:8).

Both words *straightway* and *immediately* are translated from the same Greek word *eutheos*. It has also been translated as *forthwith*. These men had an instant response to the call of the Lord. It required them to leave their comfort zones. It required them to leave their livelihood.

I understand the need to seek prayerful counsel. I understand the value of checking your actions by the integrity of the Word of God. But I also have seen and experienced the loss produced by putting things off. Procrastination has destroyed many ministries. It often disguises itself as *'prayerful caution'*. The reality is that many times our so-called caution is fear: the fear of failure, the fear of rejection, the fear of disappointments. Excuses are found to justify waiting until a more opportune time.

God's purposes are accomplished in His time, not our convenience. The first thing that I tell those seeking to enter ministry is that once they commit to do the work of the Lord, everything else becomes secondary. I am amazed at the number of people who treat ministry as a hobby. A person that is reluctant to change his schedule to obey the Lord is not fit for ministry (Luke 9:62).

REASON NUMBER THREE: FAMILY AND FRIENDS

For I know the thoughts that I think toward you, saith the LORD, thoughts of peace, and not of evil, to give you an expected end. (Jeremiah 29:11)

God called me into the ministry in 1984. I knew that I was called, but it was the most difficult thing to tell anyone else. My wife, my friends and other relatives could not see what I was seeing in my spirit. I was often frustrated and disillusioned. At times, I believed I had totally missed God. I thought that my call to the ministry was a figment of my imagination.

What I failed to realize was that others could not see my potential for looking at me. My wife saw how inconsistent I was in so many things. She endured me starting many projects, only to abandon them in midstream.

From the time we were married in 1973, I was constantly trying to start a 'hot new business'. Most of them never got off the ground or failed in their infancy. In addition, I regularly moved from job to job. I had not demonstrated any successes that could validate my consistency. No wonder she was skeptical when I declared I was called to pastor. In her mind, pastoring a church was another one of my hair-brained ideas that I would abandon when things got tough. Her skepticism was founded.

What about my friends? Surely they would see my potential. The fact is, that most of my friends only saw me as 'good ole' Timmy Kurtz'. "He always got a joke" or, "He can be so silly!" Very few took me seriously. Yes, they would give verbal assent to my ideas, but would never commit to support me in any endeavor. I simply had not presented myself as a viable person to follow.

I need to interject this. Because of the image you portrayed at various times in your life, some people will never see your potential. I am an apostle, I oversee a local church, and I have ministries around the country that seek my advice and counsel. Yet, there are many in my home town of Albion that still see me as 'good ole' Timmy Kurtz'.

How about your relatives? Your brothers, sisters, aunts, uncles, and the like know you from a different perspective. Many of them have been around you from birth. They knew you before you received the Lord. They are aware of the struggles you have had since you became saved. They have seen your good days, and your bad days. They have seen your flaws, fakes and fantasies. Kinfolk simply believe that they know the 'real' you. We want family to be our greatest allies. It is their familiarity with us that can at times be our greatest distraction.

Let me bring some balance. I am by no means advocating separation from your family. I do not mean to imply that family members won't support you in ministry. I truly do not want you to avoid or disconnect from your family because of your ministry. I just want you to understand that relatives at times can have a level of closeness and familiarity with you that can be a distraction to your calling.

There is scriptural evidence that implies that Jesus' family had some difficulty with His ministry early on. Yet, we find that James, His younger brother became an ally, an apostle, and was even martyred for His big brother Jesus. Jesus loved His family, but did not allow them to become a distraction to His purpose (Matthew 12:48-50; Mark 6:3-6).

Dr. Herbert Lockyer wrote concerning Jesus' brother James:

[James] was not a believer during our Lord's life. Along with the other children of Joseph and Mary, James did not accept the Messiahship of Jesus (Matt. 13:57; Luke 7:20,21; John 7:5). There can be no doubt, however, that he did not remain unmoved by the goodness, unselfishness and example of Christ. Living with Him for almost thirty years must have left an impact on James.[13]

Scriptural history specifically records that James, who once doubted Jesus' ministry, became a pillar in the Church at Jerusalem (Acts 12:17; 15:4-34; 21:18,19; Galatians 2:1-10). He wrote the epistle bearing his name. This man who once doubted His brother Jesus, later considered himself a 'servant of Jesus Christ' (James 1:1). It is your consistent lifestyle that garners the support of family.

REASON NUMBER FOUR:

---

[13] *ALL THE MEN OF THE BIBLE* by Herbert Lockyer, D.D., D.Litt Copyright © 1958 Zondervan Publishing House. Page 170

FAILING TO UNDERSTAND GOD'S RESPONSIBILITY

In the mid to late eighties, I often felt ignored and rejected. Inside of me was great ministry, but I felt surrounded by disappointment and defeat. It was in the midst of this that the Lord led me to Romans 8:30.

> *Moreover whom he did predestinate, them he also called: <u>and whom he</u> <u>called, them he also justified: and whom he justified, them he also</u> <u>glorified.</u> (Romans 8:30)*

I realized if God had called me, it was His responsibility to justify that calling. I did not have to prove my calling to anyone. That was God's responsibility. I also realized that my anxiety and disobedience could potentially sabotage God's purpose for my life.

Instead of blaming others for rejecting my ministry, I recognized that God needed to correct 'me' in many areas. I had to become stable and focused before my wife and children. I had to stop using silliness and clowning as a way to 'garner' friends. My relatives had to see me living a consistent holy lifestyle.

I am thankful that God kept me out of sight *'tending another man's sheep'* as a choir director, during this season. His mercy did not allow an unfocused – goofy – up one day, down the next – immature kid come forth with His anointing.

Look at the results. Today, my wife is my greatest earthly ally. Friends who saw me transition from 'silly Timmy' to an apostle of the Living God now work diligently in my church. Many of my relatives recognize what God has done in my life, and some even attend and are active in my church. I give glory to God. I take no credit for His wonderful acts in my behalf.

My friend, during those times that you feel ignored and rejected, recognize that it is God who called you, and that it is God who will produce that calling. Relax in the Lord. He has your life under control. He knows how to manifest the plans that He has for your life in due season.

Chapter 6

Principle 2

You Are Not Indespensible

YOU MAY BE ANOINTED TO DO WHAT SOMEONE ELSE REFUSED TO DO!

Several years ago, I was in prayer when the Lord clearly said to me, *"I will remove you if you take credit for anything that I do at John 3:16 Ministries"*.[14] I immediately realized that I am simply an earthen vessel being used by God (2Corinthians 4:7).

Even though I am the founder and serve as the senior elder, its existence is not contingent upon me. From that day forward, I have handled the things of the Lord cautiously. I thoroughly understand that His anointing comes with a price.

---

[14] John 3:16 Ministries was the original name of New Life Ministries International

Saul never learned this lesson. The Berkley Version[15] of the bible describes Saul as 'young and well built'. The Knox Translation[16] says that Saul was 'a fine figure of a man'. His good looks and physical appearance became the image the people wanted in a leader. He became king of Israel by the will of the people, not the will of God (1Samuel 8:6,7). Saul let this go to his head. It never occurred to him that he became king, because the people had rejected God

Saul started well but soon became a habitual failure. He would disobey God, and then blame the people for his failure (1Samuel 15:15). He always had an excuse. He became so reprobate near the end of his life that he consulted a witch for advice (1Samuel 28:7). God rejected him from being King over Israel because of his rebellion (1Samuel 15:26). His life ended in suicide (1Samuel 31:4).

> Then Samuel took the horn of oil, and anointed him in the midst of his brethren: and the spirit of the LORD came upon David from that day forward. So Samuel rose up, and went to Ramah. But the spirit of the LORD departed from Saul, and an evil spirit from the LORD troubled him. (1Samuel 16:13-14)

---

[15] (First Samuel 9:2) *The Modern Language Bible: The New Berkley Version in Modern English*, Copyright © 1945, 1959, 1969 by Zondervan Publishing House.

[16] (First Samuel 9:2) *The Holy Bible: A Translation from the Latin Vulgate in the Light of the Hebrew and Greek Originals* by Monsignor Ronald Knox. Copyright © 1954 by Sheed and Ward, Inc., New York, with the kind permission of His Eminence, the Cardinal Archbishop of Westminster and Burns and Oates, LTD.

As Saul was being rejected by God, little unknown David was tending his father's sheep. David had no clue as to the awesome transfer that was about to change his life.

Samuel poured oil on David to anoint him as king. Simultaneously as David received the Spirit of the Lord, Saul lost the Spirit of the Lord. Don't miss this point. Whatever gift you have is from the Lord. If you fail to use it properly, God has those who will. The calling you have on your life could be a result of someone else failing to fulfill theirs.

If some of the branches have been broken off, and you, though a wild olive shoot, have been grafted in among the others and now share in the nourishing sap from the olive root, do not boast over those branches. If you do, consider this: You do not support the root, but the root supports you. You will say then, "Branches were broken off so that I could be grafted in." Granted. But they were broken off because of unbelief, and you stand by faith. Do not be arrogant, but be afraid. For if God did not spare the natural branches, he will not spare you either. (Romans 11:17-21 New International Version)

Have you ever considered the impact that Israel's rejection of Jesus Christ had on you? They were God's original chosen people. They were chosen not to rule the world, but to be a light to the Gentiles through whom all nations would be blessed (Luke 2:32; Galatians 3:8). Like Saul, they often misinterpreted God's purpose for their nation. As a result, they rejected Jesus Christ, because they did not recognize Him as the Messiah (Matthew 27:25; John 19:14,15; 1Peter 2:7,8)

When Israel rejected Jesus Christ, God rejected them. They were cut off, and we were grafted in. No longer is one a Jew by outward circumcision, but one is a Jew by circumcision of the heart (Romans 2:28,29). You and I are Jews, the seed of Abraham by faith in Jesus Christ (Galatians 3:26-29). The message is clear—if you reject Jesus Christ, you too will be cut off from the root.

None of us is indispensable. There are some, who mistakenly believe that the purposes of God will suffer if they aren't in place. Romans 11:21 proves this is not true. Scripture clearly teaches us that God resists the proud (James 4:6).

Those who build their ministries around themselves are in danger of being cutoff due to pride (Matthew 7:22,23; 1Corinthians 3:11-15). Contrary to what they may believe, God will cut them off, and the ministry they thought they had will flourish. Any branch that does not produce, God purges it so that the tree can bear more fruit (John 15:2).

YOUR POSITION IS NOT
A REFLECTION OF YOUR ANOINTING

Your position in life, or in the church, does not mean that you are anointed of God. In a position, you may have the ability to exercise certain authority. But it is also possible that people may honor a position, but loathe the one who is in it.

Saul remained king over Israel approximately thirteen years after God had rejected him. He was depressed, angry, bitter and jealous (1Samuel 16:14; 18:8). He spent most of his reign chasing David. Yet, he held the mantle of king.

> *Then gathered the chief priests and the Pharisees a council, and said, What do we? for this man doeth many miracles. If we let him thus alone, all men will believe on him: and the Romans shall come and take away both our place and nation. (John 11:47-48)*

The chief priests and the Pharisees held positions of authority. Under covenant law they had the right to perform certain rituals in the Temple. Under Temple Law they could invoke certain laws and requirements that affected the people. They took their positions as a sign that they had special privileges with God.

When Jesus came to their territory, the Pharisees were not concerned as to whether He was right or wrong. Their concern was that Jesus' ministry would cause the Romans to take away their 'positions'.

The position you hold in life is from God. You can be the president of the choir or the President of the United States (Romans 13:1). The authority that is allowed only reflects the perimeters allowed by the position. It does not reflect your anointing. Like Saul, people can put you in a position, but only God can anoint you for it.

YOUR GIFT WILL NOT OVERRIDE CHARACTER FLAWS

In the church, we have allowed people to believe that 'any success' proves that they are anointed of God. One accurate prophecy makes them a prophet. One person healed gives them a healing ministry. Churches have often prematurely elevated such people to leadership positions. Unfortunately, that individual is fooled into believing that their '*spiritual performance*' validates them.

The Apostle Paul had to aggressively deal with this issue of gifts versus character in the Corinthian church. They were instructed so that they would 'come behind in no gift' (1Corinthians 1:7). They were a church that was filled with 'spiritual gifts'. They could do it all. But they tolerated immorality (1Corinthians 5:1). No calling of God can override sin. Paul wrote that the 'gifts and calling are without repentance' (Romans 11:29). This should by no means imply that sin should be overlooked and ignored.

> *But Jesus said unto them, A prophet is not without honour, but in his own country, and among his own kin, and in his own house. And he could there do no mighty work, save that he laid his hands upon a few sick folk, and healed them. And he marvelled because of their unbelief. And he went round about the villages, teaching. (Mark 6:4-6)*

I have heard people use Mark 6:4 as an excuse to override their character flaws. They imply that their ministry is not accepted by those around them because of envy and jealousy. Ironically, these people are often well accepted outside of their immediate area but at home, around kin and acquaintances, they have a horrible testimony.

They have no respect in the business community because of how they handle their financial matters. They have no respect among church leadership because they will not submit to biblical authority. Their family has little or no respect because of their inconsistent lifestyles.

Jesus was not accepted in his hometown because of *their* unbelief – not His character. He could not perform many miracles because of *their* unbelief – not because He lived a questionable and inconsistent lifestyle.

But ye shall receive power, after that the Holy Ghost is come upon you: <u>and ye shall be witnesses unto me both in Jerusalem, and in all Judaea, and in Samaria, and unto the uttermost part of the earth.</u> (Acts 1:8)

Acts 1:8 is a prototype of calling, ministry and purpose. You will see how important your character is in this process.

Through the Holy Ghost, we are given power to be witnesses. Being a witness is a universal calling for all believers. How we witness will vary from individual to individual. However your witness will be greatly impacted by your character.

Jesus introduces us to three dimensions of witnessing – Jerusalem, Judea, Samaria and the uttermost parts of the world. He did not say that we should be witnesses only in the uttermost parts of the world, but in three dimensions that qualify us for worldwide ministry. Let's take a closer look at what He is saying to us.

Your first witness is in your *Jerusalem*. This represents your home territory. *It is the witness you have around the people that truly know you.* It is ministry among those who have seen you in success and failure. It is ministry among those who may in fact choose to reject you for personal reasons. That rejection should be because of their unbelief, and not your character flaws.

I oversee a church in the same city where I have lived my entire life. It is a small community where everybody knows everybody. I pastor people that knew my parents before I was born. I pastor people I went to school with. I pastor people who partied with me before I was saved. God anointed me to do this work. My character and public lifestyle undergirds the work He does through me (1Corinthians 9:27).

Your second witness is in your *Judaea*. This is a type of the region around you. *This is the witness you have among those who know you through someone else.* Some people may not know you personally, but when they hear your name, they know the character that is associated with it.

A good name is rather to be chosen than great riches, and loving favour rather than silver and gold. (Proverbs 22:1)

Never under estimate the value of your name. Your name is more than what identifies you. It is often the first mental image a person will have of you. Your name is often attached to a description of who you are.

Think for a moment. There are individuals whose name evokes an immediate reaction in you. When you hear some names, they may produce joy in you. Yet, other names create anxiety and anger. Those individuals may be nowhere near you, but the mere mention of their name produces an internal response from you.

Your name does the same thing. Jesus asked His disciples what they and other people were saying about Him (Matthew 16:13-15). Have you ever seriously considered what others say or think about you? Whatever they think, it is your name that triggers those thoughts.

It will be those in your *Jerusalem* that will carry your name into your *Judaea* (Matthew 4:24; 9:26; 14:1; Mark 7:36; Luke 8:39). The effectiveness of your ministry will be directly linked to the name you have built for yourself. Look around you. You are surrounded by those who are comfortable or antagonized by your name.

You can tell as much about yourself by who avoids you, as you do by those who hang around you. If the right people avoid you, and the wrong people attach themselves to you – you may have a problem. Watch those who will use your name to validate their integrity. Good character never needs a cosigner.

If you are trustworthy and honest, that name will precede you. If you are loving and caring, that name will precede you. Those in your *Judaea* may not know you personally, but they will receive from you, based on the name you have.

Your third witness is to your *Samaria*. This represents a type of ministry among people that you dislike – and that equally dislike you. The Jews hated the Samaritans, yet Jesus expected His disciples to minister among them. He set the example when He ministered to the Samaritan woman at the well (John 4:9).

You enter Samaria by choice. You reach out to former enemies and distracters because of their need for Jesus Christ. You may find that misunderstandings were in fact *understandings that you missed*.

Whatever ministry God has placed in you is for His glory, not yours. You may be rejected or hated by people, but never refuse to share His love through your gifts and calling among them. Your purpose should always be to win them to Jesus Christ. It is not until you have been through your *Jerusalem, Judaea* and *Samaria* that you qualify to minister throughout the world.

Ask yourself this question. "If by chance, one of those I've ministered to outside my immediate area should visit me without notice, would they find the same person at home that they met on the road?" "If they should ask my friends, relatives and enemies about me, would they hear a consistent testimony of my good character?"

Value your character. Don't believe that you are invincible. Please don't believe that God can't get the job done without you (1Kings 19:18). You are only a vessel being used by God (2Corinthians 4:7). Whatever gifts you have, God has given them to you for His glory. Use them to win the lost, not create your own personal kingdom.

Chapter 7

Principle 3
Guard Your Heart

YOUR HEART AND ACTIONS IN ANOTHER MAN'S MINISTRY
PRODUCES THE REWARDS IN YOUR OWN!

Keep thy heart with all diligence; for out of it are the issues of life.
(Proverbs 4:23)

When Samuel came to seek a king, David was tending his father's sheep. It seemed as though David spent the early part of his life working for someone else – even after he was anointed to be the king! He was a musician (1Samuel 16:23). He wrote most of the songbook of the bible – Psalms. Yet, he began his musical career playing music for one man that at times hated him.

Whenever Saul had a bad day, they called David to play music to calm him down (1Samuel 16:15-19). King Saul was so emotionally disturbed that he once even tried to kill David while he was playing (1Samuel 18:10,11). What a way to start a musical career. Throughout this ordeal, the bible says that David 'behaved himself wisely' (1Samuel 18:14).

David served King Saul as his armor bearer (1Samuel 16:21). This was a significant 'servant' role. It was more than just carrying the king's armor. The armor bearer lived daily with their life on the line.

"...the King James word armourbearer was translated from two Hebrew words. The first is *nasa* or *nacah (naw-saw')*. This is a primary word meaning "to *lift.*" It has a great variety of applications, both figuratively and literally. Some of the more interesting applications are to: accept, advance, bear, bear up, carry away, cast, desire, furnish, further, give, help, hold up, lift, pardon, raise, regard, respect, stir up, yield.

The second Hebrew word is *keliy (kel-ee'),* which comes from the root word *kalah (kaw-law'),* meaning "to *end.*" Some of the applications of this root word are to: complete, consume, destroy utterly, be done, finish, fulfill, long, bring to pass, wholly reap, make clean riddance.

From these two Hebrew words, we can see the duty of the armor bearer was to stand beside the leader to assist him, to lift him up, and to protect him against any enemy that might attack him.[17]

As you pursue your vision and dreams this is an important lesson to learn. *What ever you do in another man's ministry will become the seed that produces the harvest in your own.*

There will be times that you may feel 'used' by those over you. You feel that you do all the work, and they get all the credit. You aren't even recognized when great accolades are being given to the one you have served faithfully. If you allow bitterness and anger to creep in, you are pushing the self-destruct button on your own ministry aspirations.

At the time of this writing, my daughter is an executive in a local bank. She was hired, in part, because at twenty-three years of age, she already had significant banking experience. How did this happen?

It began in high school. There, she chose to enter an administrative clerical program in the county's vocational school. This opened the door for her to become a receptionist in the loan department of a local credit union. At seventeen, she took this job with great enthusiasm. Soon, the other 'experienced' workers in the loan department began to dump their unwanted work on her. Rather than complain about the increased workload, she eagerly completed each task assigned.

---

[17] *GOD'S ARMORBEARER: How To Serve God's Leaders* Copyright © 1990 by Terry Nance – Published by Harrison House, Inc.

The 'unwanted work' taught her about the workings of a loan department. She became so proficient in her skills, that for a while, she was given the responsibility to review all loan applications for compliance to various federal and state lending regulations. By the time she was nineteen, she had been promoted to Loan Officer – the youngest that credit union had ever had.

When the opportunity came for her current position, she had attained a wealth of information and experience. Her attitude in the early days when others were dumping extra work on her became the seed for the harvest she is reaping today.

I have counseled many people who complained that they are forced to do things on their job that is not in their job description. They felt that they were being taken advantage of. It is that mentality that will keep you from ever attaining any growth. Let me give you some practical advice.

> He that is faithful in that which is least is faithful also in much: and he
> that is unjust in the least is unjust also in much. If therefore ye have not
> been faithful in the unrighteous mammon, who will commit to your trust
> the true riches? And if ye have not been faithful in that which is another
> man's, who shall give you that which is your own? (Luke 16:10-12)

The Word of God is clear. Your faithfulness in another man's ministry will produce victory in your own. Wherever you are serving at this time, do it to give glory unto the Lord (1Corinthians 10:31).

If you are working in a company, do everything in your power to make that company successful. If you are a factory worker, do everything you can to insure the best products are produced. If you are working in your church, do everything you can to cause that ministry to succeed.

> *For God is not unrighteous to forget your work and labour of love, which ye have showed toward his name, in that ye have ministered to the saints, and do minister. (Hebrews 6:10)*

1. GO THE EXTRA MILE

Whenever you are asked to go beyond what you were hired to do, determine how it will effect your primary function and use the additional task as a learning tool. I teach a principle, "The more you know – the more you grow". You may not need what you learn now, but it could be vital to you in the future.

2. DON'T COMPLAIN

Sometimes additional work will cause stress, but you control your attitude. If you don't believe you can accomplish the additional work within the timeframe given, make that clear to your supervisor. However, offer solutions to accomplish the task. Don't just refuse to do it.

3. PROVIDE SOLUTIONS

Others may dump their unwanted task on you, but your ability to provide solutions will always work in your favor. You position yourself for promotion, when you own the solution.

4. CONTROL YOUR ATTITUDE

Remember the Godly attitude. Don't' work simply to be seen of men, but to be pleasing to God (Ephesians 6:5-8; Colossians 3:22-25).

Chapter 8

Principle 4
Be Responsible...

BE RESPONSIBLE. RESPONSIBILITY IS THE FOUNDATION OF CONFIDENCE.

The fourth principle to understand is that of being responsible. Responsibility is the *foundation* of confidence. No one can succeed in any endeavor if they have not first learned what it means to be responsible.

There are two sides to responsibility. First, you must *maintain responsibility* which is to insure that established duties and commitments are fulfilled. Second, you must *take responsibility* for your actions and decisions in the pursuit of anything you do. David both *maintained responsibility* and *took responsibility* to earn the confidence of his father and Saul.

> *And the three eldest sons of Jesse went and followed Saul to the battle: and the names of his three sons that went to the battle were Eliab the firstborn, and next unto him Abinadab, and the third Shammah. And David was the youngest: and the three eldest followed Saul. But David went and returned from Saul to feed his father's sheep at Bethlehem. (1Samuel 17:13-15)*

David had a short stint in the palace working for Saul. But when a conflict broke out between Israel and the Philistines, he was sent back home to his old job as a shepherd in his father's fields.

One day, you are in the spotlight, the next day you are in obscurity. In the minds of many, this would be a demotion.

I want you to see how David handled this situation. Everyone around him still saw him as the kid that *'watched his daddy's sheep'*. David took this job seriously.

> *And Jesse said unto David his son, Take now for thy brethren an ephah of this parched corn, and these ten loaves, and run to the camp to thy brethren; And carry these ten cheeses unto the captain of their thousand, and look how thy brethren fare, and take their pledge. (1Samuel 17:17-18)*

Once again David was called while tending sheep in the field. This time, he was given a temporary assignment to take food to his brothers. This menial job could have been done by any of Jesse's hired servants. What a roller coaster ride this was for David!

He started in the fields with the sheep, and the next thing he knew a prophet was anointing him to be king of Israel. He gets a trip to the palace to play for the king, only to be sent back to the fields when war broke out. Now he's being called again, to take food to brothers who were obviously considered more valuable than he. It is in times and situations like this that your true heart for success will be tested.

Many people fail because they allow their feelings to dictate their actions. They don't like being up today and down tomorrow. They allow themselves to be embarrassed by what they perceive as 'being used'. Instead of responding with responsible actions, they try to manipulate their way back to a position of prominence. Let's see what David did.

> *And David rose up early in the morning, and left the sheep with a keeper, and took, and went, as Jesse had commanded him... (1Samuel 17:20)*

> *And David left his carriage in the hand of the keeper of the carriage, and ran into the army, and came and saluted his brethren. (1Samuel 17:22)*

David was given an assignment from his father to take food to his brothers. He also had the responsibility of caring for his father's sheep. He could have taken off, simply seeking for an opportunity to get close to the king again. He could have viewed this as his opportunity to prove himself once and for all.

Instead, David maintained responsibility of his father's sheep. He waited until the next morning when he had arranged for someone to keep them while he fulfilled his assignment. He also took the same care to protect his father's carriage by leaving it in the care of the carriage keeper. These two acts are prime examples of maintaining responsibility for current tasks when new assignments arise.

David did not know what was before him. He was not aware of his impending conflict with Goliath. He did not go expecting Saul to deputize him for battle. He fully expected to deliver the food to his brothers and then return to his duties as a shepherd.

Most of us have tasks that are considered our primary responsibility. Occasionally, a temporary assignment comes along that will temporarily draw us away from our primary duties. To pass the test of 'success', you must first past the test of *maintaining and taking responsibility*. You must never relinquish the care and responsibility of those things that really matter. New assignments are an opportunity – not your destiny.

Maintaining responsibility dictates that your first obligation is to insure that your primary duties are sustained in your absence. It is during these temporary assignments that access to your destiny can be revealed. If you accomplish the temporary assignment with flying colors, and your primary responsibilities suffer, you have failed. You will be judged by how well you handle your primary duties, not by your temporary assignments.

This is critical. Many have 'succeeded' in ministry, but their families were dysfunctional and defeated. Many have 'succeeded' in business, and left a trail of moral failure. Hollywood is filled with those who can masquerade as worldly 'success' while living in depression, fear and anxiety. Politicians have been elected by popularity and defeated by immorality everyday. People have unwittingly placed confidence in those that don't take responsibility for their corrupt actions.

Several years ago, the Lord confirmed in my spirit that my *'anointing is in the unusual'*. I am often led to pursue uncharted territory in accomplishing the Lord's work for me. I am an apostolic pioneer. Admittedly, I am often uncomfortable doing what I do. In the quest for the unusual, I must maintain consistency and order in my church. While finding ways to establish new values and processes to transition the church to a New Testament structure, it is critical to maintain stability for those who have not understood or embraced the change. My brother, Joseph put it best when he said, "While pursuing the unusual, you must be able keep the usual in order."

When you *take responsibility*, you commit to being accountable for the outcome of any decision or action you make. You recognize what others may say or do to you as a result of your actions or decisions. To take responsibility is to be aware of things you do or say that produce negative outcomes in your life. This is difficult for many to understand. I am often asked, "Why should I take responsibility for what someone else does to me?"

This question is a result of misunderstanding the difference between taking responsibility and taking the blame. Taking responsibility is not taking the blame for what someone else may do to you. It is to clearly understand your role in triggering their reaction. It is being cognizant of *your actions*, and not their response. This is not to paint yourself into a corner of guilt, but rather an opportunity for you to recognize patterns that impact your life.

A few years ago I was counseling a man who was about to be divorced – for the fourth time! According to him, his wife was the worst woman in the world, yet a year or so earlier she was the best thing God had created. This had been the same story in his previous three marriages. He had married the best woman in the world only to end up divorcing her a few years later. As he and I discussed his latest divorce, I stated that I had found a common denominator that would resolve his marital woes. He was greatly dismayed to find that he was the common denominator. Four different women could not all be as wrong as he painted them. Somewhere along the line he had to take responsibility for his actions in the marriage.

If you are experiencing the similar responses from many people it may indicate something about you – rather than them. In other words, if someone calls you a donkey – get mad. If two people call you a donkey – you may end up in a fight. If three people call you a donkey – buy a saddle! Reoccurring patterns are a sign that you may not be taking responsibility. Taking responsibility empowers you to make changes. As long as you blame others for your plight in life, they will always control your destiny.

Do you see the destiny God has for you? Do you regularly face similar obstacles? If so, be responsible. Do an assessment of what you say, or actions you take. If you are really courageous, allow others you trust to speak into your life to alert you to things you do to sabotage your future. Remember that your future is not at the expense of your present. What God has for you tomorrow does not erase what He has entrusted you with today. Be responsible.

Principle 5

Be Aware of Your Surroundings

OPPORTUNITY COMES TO THOSE WHO ARE AWARE OF THEIR SURROUNDINGS!

Closely linked to being responsible is being aware. When you take and maintain responsibility, your mind is clear to see and accurately interpret the activities and events around you. David was near the battlefront to deliver food to his brothers, but yet he was able to see and assess the current state of the battle.

If David had failed to maintain responsibility of his father's sheep and carriage, his motives may have been more to position himself for what he may have perceived as a lofty position. His sight would have been focused on himself, rather than the purposes of the Lord. Both David and the Israeli army saw the same thing, but perceived two different things.

And there went out a champion out of the camp of the Philistines, named Goliath, of Gath, whose height was six cubits and a span. And he had an helmet of brass upon his head, and he was armed with a coat of mail; and the weight of the coat was five thousand shekels of brass. And he had greaves of brass upon his legs, and a target of brass between his shoulders. And the staff of his spear was like a weaver's beam; and his spear's head weighed six hundred shekels of iron: and one bearing a shield went before him. And he stood and cried unto the armies of Israel, and said unto them, Why are ye come out to set your battle in array? am not I a Philistine, and ye servants to Saul? choose you a man for you, and let him come down to me. If he be able to fight with me, and to kill me, then will we be your servants: but if I prevail against him, and kill him, then shall ye be our servants, and serve us. And the Philistine said, I defy the armies of Israel this day; give me a man, that we may fight together. When Saul and all Israel heard those words of the Philistine, they were dismayed, and greatly afraid. (1Samuel 17:4-11)

And the Philistine drew near morning and evening, and presented himself forty days. (1Samuel 17:16)

And as [David] talked with them, behold, there came up the champion, the Philistine of Gath, Goliath by name, out of the armies of the

Philistines, and spake according to the same words: and David heard them. And all the men of Israel, when they saw the man, fled from him, and were sore afraid. And the men of Israel said, Have ye seen this man that is come up? surely to defy Israel is he come up: and it shall be, that the man who killeth him, the king will enrich him with great riches, and will give him his daughter, and make his father's house free in Israel. And David spake to the men that stood by him, saying, What shall be done to the man that killeth this Philistine, and taketh away the reproach from Israel? for who is this uncircumcised Philistine, that he should defy the armies of the living God? And the people answered him after this manner, saying, So shall it be done to the man that killeth him. (1Samuel 17:23-27)

David's *responsibility* was the care of his father's sheep. His *temporary assignment* was to carry food to his brothers. It was in the midst of his assignment that Goliath presented himself. For forty days Goliath had taunted Israel, and for forty days, Israel had fled from him.

The mere sight of this giant was intimidating. Based on information gleaned from scripture (1Samuel 17:4), Goliath was at least 9 ½ feet tall and perhaps as tall as 11 feet. The magnificence of Goliath's armor and weapons—his bronze coat of mail, bronze greaves, bronze javelin, spear with an iron spearhead, and huge sword—must have made him appear invincible.[18]

---

[18] GOLIATH *Nelson's Illustrated Bible Dictionary* Copyright © 1986 by Thomas Nelson Publishers –page 437

What made David different from everyone else? I believe the answer is in the last four words of First Samuel 17:23 *"...and David heard them"*. Goliath's taunting words had a different sound to David.

The Israeli army heard a giant whose words seem to validate his strength. David heard the words of an uncircumcised enemy of God who had no right to his claims (1Samuel 17:26). Israel heard the words of a giant with years of battle experience. David heard the threats of one that he deemed to be less than an animal (1Samuel 17:36).

In the midst of doing your assignment, be aware of all that is happening around you. Listen to the attitude of others. You may discover that your assignment has given you access to key situations and people. Your assignment may be the avenue that will propel you into your next season. You can miss opportunities if you view your assignment as just another task to be done.

Other than his brothers, David had no real and direct connection to the battle. He could have simply dropped off the food and gone home. Or, he could have used this time to promote himself. When Goliath taunted Israel, David could have simply said 'it was none of his business' and left.

It is interesting that the army had been taunted for forty days by Goliath, and in a few moments David ascertained a completely different perspective. In the midst of his assignment he recognized a problem that no one was willing to solve. As everyone else ran, David began to ask questions. He quickly determined that whoever killed Goliath, would in fact take away the reproach of Israel.

Problem solving is a foundational principle of success. You have no doubt heard the cliché, '*find a need and fill it*'. The solutions to most problems are discovered from totally unrelated task. Imagine how many solutions have been delayed or missed because someone was afraid to ask the right questions.

CONFRONT THE ISSUES

David quickly saw that Israel was in a one-sided shouting match. The score was Goliath forty, and the home team zero. Simply put, the home team needed a knockout punch. However, nobody on the home team, including the king, wanted to get in the ring with the giant. Incentives hadn't produced any takers. Saul had offered riches, his daughter, prestige and the right to live tax free to whoever would kill Goliath – but there were no takers.

David's motivation was not for personal gain. He saw Israel being ridiculed. He saw the people of God being intimidated. He never made mention of the rewards he could receive, he only saw his people being verbally defeated every day. His assignment would have given him legitimate excuse to ignore what he saw. The taunts of the giant could have fallen on spiritually deaf ears. He had every right to respond in fear like every one else had over the previous forty days.

Fear will paralyze you. Your destiny will be held hostage by the thing you are afraid to confront. There is a time when you must face the giant. You must see through the giant into your destiny and be willing to act. Giants will distract you. They often appear when you are completing an assignment. We will discuss later how they operate, but for now you need to recognize their purpose is to stop you from moving forward.

In a previous episode, Israel succumbed to the giants near the borders of Canaan.

> We came unto the land whither thou sentest us, and surely it floweth with milk and honey; and this is the fruit of it. <u>Nevertheless the people be strong that dwell in the land, and the cities are walled, and very great: and moreover we saw the children of Anak there.</u> The Amalekites dwell in the land of the south: and the Hittites, and the Jebusites, and the Amorites, dwell in the mountains: and the Canaanites dwell by the sea, and by the coast of Jordan. And Caleb stilled the people before Moses, and said, Let us go up at once, and possess it; for we are well able to overcome it. But the men that went up with him said, We be not able to go up against the people; for they are stronger than we. And they brought up an evil report of the land which they had searched unto the children of Israel, saying, The land, through which we have gone to search it, is a land that eateth up the inhabitants thereof; and all the people that we saw in it are men of a great stature. <u>And there we saw the giants, the sons of Anak, which come of the giants: and we were in our own sight as grasshoppers, and so we were in their sight.</u> (Numbers 13:27-33)

In their first confrontation Israel made three damaging assumptions: they perceived the sons of Anak to be giants, they saw themselves as grasshoppers and assumed the sons of Anak saw them the same. Their miscalculation doomed them to forty years in the wilderness. Generations later this fear was clearly still resident in them as they ran forty days from Goliath. If you are internally motivated by fear, you may see something too large to attempt to confront and find yourself running from the very thing God has allowed to promote you.

What is your current assignment? What giants have you encountered while doing it? What dreams have they told you were impossible? How long have you been in the valley being taunted by the giants of failure? Get up my friend! It's time to go forth. The very fact that you have encountered a giant is proof that you have reached the borders of your promised land. Either you face the giant, or run like Israel.

When you become aware of your surroundings, you will often see things from a different perspective than those in the midst of the arena. Your view is filtered through your internal motivations and perceptions. You may see a problem that needs to be solved, or you may see an opportunity for self-promotion. Ironically, outwardly they may look the same, but the eternal results will be vastly different.

If the opportunist faces a giant, they are more apt to attempt negotiating with him. Yes, they want to win, but they want to look good in the process. The opportunist is willing to compromise with the giant to bolster their own image. They would give the giant permanent rights and would allow them levels of oppression upon the weak. At the same time, they would hypocritically declare to the weak that they have their best interest in mind.

Those who seek to solve problems faced by the weak will have no mercy on the giant. They are willing to put their own life at risk in order to protect them. That's what David did. He saw Israel being taunted by Goliath, and as you will read later, he put his life on the line in order to eliminate him.

Chapter 10

Principle 6

Beware of Distractions

DISTRACTIONS COME TO DELAY, DISCOURAGE AND
ULTIMATELY DESTROY YOU.

It's amazing that distractions will often come from those who should
be your supporters. I often teach that *if satan can't get you with sin, he will
destroy you with distraction.* The satanic design of distraction is to cause
you to miss your destiny. If you can be drawn away from your primary
purposes it increases the possibility of failure.

There are both negative and what appear to be positive
distractions that you will face. The negative distractions come to
intimidate you. The seemingly positive distractions appeal to your

carnal desires. This is one reason the Apostle Paul warned us to flee youthful lusts and pursue righteousness (2Timothy 2:22).

When David arrived at the battle scene, Israel was emotionally defeated. Rather than become absorbed in the collective fear, he chose to speak out against the Philistine giant. It would seem that there would be an immediate positive response. Instead he was rebuked by his own blood brother.

And Eliab his eldest brother heard when he spake unto the men; and Eliab's anger was kindled against David, and he said, Why camest thou down hither? and with whom hast thou left those few sheep in the wilderness? I know thy pride, and the naughtiness of thine heart; for thou art come down that thou mightest see the battle. (1Samuel 17:28)

Relatives, friends, co-workers can at times say things that cut deep into your heart. Consider for a moment the position of Eliab. He was David's oldest brother. In that culture he was first in line to receive a double portion of an inheritance from his father Jesse. Being the oldest, I am sure the other brothers looked to him for advice and strength. Yet, like all of Israel, he was cowering under the threats of Goliath.

Eliab had worn his armor and carried his weapons for forty days. He had looked tough, but he was as fearful as the rest of the army. Like those around him, he had most likely complained about Goliath, but never offered any solutions to his threats. It must have been embarrassing to Eliab to have his baby brother show up and start asking questions. Maybe he wanted to protect his baby brother from being hurt. Maybe he intended to scare his kid brother off. Maybe he felt his status as the oldest brother in his family would intimidate David and send him running home to daddy. Or maybe, deep inside he resented David for being anointed by Samuel and this was his opportunity to get back at him.

Eliab also seemed to have a low view of his father's sheep and David's ability to care for them. By referring to his father's sheep as "...*those few sheep*" he exposed that he placed little value on his father's property, and no confidence in David. People who come to distract you usually place little or no value on anything that matters to you.

David however, was focused. He knew his temporary assignment was to deliver cheese to his brothers and in the midst of this mission he became aware of Goliath. He simply began to ask questions and his oldest brother Eliab quickly became his first potential distracter.

Distracters have their motives, but their purpose is always the same – to turn you away from your destiny. Some distractions appear more appealing. I have seen churches fall apart because the pastor was distracted by a money making scheme they thought would increase their finances. I have seen marriages crumble because another person or other things took priority. I have seen potentially great ministers lose focus running after things they thought would make them succeed.

This kind of distraction will appear viable for a moment. What may look like an opportunity often becomes a costly burden that consumes financial, emotional and spiritual resources meant for the journey to your true destiny.

CONSIDER JESUS

And the devil, taking him up into an high mountain, shewed unto him all the kingdoms of the world in a moment of time. And the devil said unto him, All this power will I give thee, and the glory of them: for that is delivered unto me; and to whomsoever I will I give it. If thou therefore wilt worship me, all shall be thine. (Luke 4:5-7)

In the wilderness, satan offered Jesus all the kingdoms of the world if he would simply bow down and worship him. This was more than a simple temptation. It was a major distraction – both negative and positive. Let's consider the magnitude of satan's offer?

Jesus knew His purpose for coming to the earth. He came to bear witness of the truth (John 18:37). He came to destroy the works of the devil (1 John 3:8). He came to save that which was lost (Matthew 18:11; Luke 19:10). He came to do the will of the Father (John 4:34; 6:38; 6:40).

Jesus was also well aware that He came to die on the cross (Matthew 16:21; John 12:27). Through the suffering of the cross, He would totally defeat satan (Colossians 2:15). Through the suffering of the cross He would be given authority and all power in heaven and earth (Matthew 28:18; 1Corinthians 15:24,25). Jesus knew that ultimately, through the suffering of the cross, all kingdoms of this world would submit to Him (Revelation 11:15).

The cross could have been a powerful negative distraction to Jesus. The fear of such a horrendous death could have made Him make wrong decisions. With all the emotional agony He must have endured, He chose the will of the Father (Matthew 26:38,39; Hebrews 12:2). The devil therefore offered a more appealing distraction. When he offered Jesus the kingdoms of the world, he was giving Him the opportunity to by-pass the cross.

Jesus knew that the kingdoms of this world, would become the Kingdom of our God and of his Christ (Revelation 11:15). The offer satan made to Jesus was to receive the world's kingdoms with a bow, rather than the cross.

Many times distractions will appear as an easier path to your destiny. What may appear to be a shortcut may in fact be a trap. There are two ways to avoid distraction.

First, know who you are. Spend time with the Lord. Confront your weaknesses and flaws with honesty before the Lord. The devil will try to use your weakness to attack your strengths. Many times shortcuts are offers that will keep you from confronting an issue that is defeating you.

In 1987, when I first felt that I was called to pastor, I began to share my vision with several people – but unfortunately I strategically did not share my vision with my pastor. One particular ministry acquaintance offered to help me get started. He promised to donate sound equipment, chairs and money to help me open a church. He felt that I should 'seize the moment'. God had called me, so he encouraged me to act upon it immediately. He even claimed to have had a vision of the same building that I was considering for the church.

Later, I felt led to contact a man about some property he owned and had for sale. I asked him to consider donating his three-unit apartment house to us so that we would have income in our church from day one. At the time I made this contact, he and his wife were looking for a Spirit-filled church, and he felt my contact with him may have been an answer to his prayers. He agreed to prayerfully consider my request.

"This is great", I thought. The building, the equipment and possibly even a source of income were being provided to me. I began to secretly make plans to start a church. The way things were moving, I was sure that 'all things were working together for my good'.

One day as I was driving home from work, the Lord spoke to me about this matter as clear as I have ever heard Him. "This is not of me, leave it alone!" I was stunned. It seemed like everything was falling into place. The building, equipment and the money had to have been from God. Yet, I knew from the voice of God in my spirit that this was not the path I was to take.

In reluctant obedience, I began to back off from the arrangements I had made. The building owner shrugged off my cancellation to lease his building for the church as just another business deal gone sour. Later I learned that the building I wanted to use was not zoned to house a church. We would have had tremendous opposition trying to use it for that purpose.

The man who was considering donating the income from his apartment house was a gracious Spirit-filled Christian. He thanked me for 'hearing from the Lord'. Ironically, two years later, he and I served together as elders in a local church. My wife and I have purchased two properties from him since then, and we remain good friends with him and his wife today.

The ministry acquaintance who offered to donate the chairs and sound equipment became angry when I backed out. He accused me of being weak and fearful. Today, he is divorced and horribly backslidden.

Providing for honest things, not only in the sight of the Lord, but also in the sight of men. (2Corinthians 8:21)

As for me, I realized that my actions were deceptive. I had purposely withheld information regarding my plans from my Pastor. If they had materialized as I thought they would, I would have left the church with little or no warning. I was a minister, musician and director of the young adult choir. How unfair this would have been just to walk out without notice to *do the work of the Lord*.

Anytime God gives you something to do it is unnecessary and wrong to be deceptive. By withholding information from my Pastor, I had to move towards my plans dishonestly. I was not respecting the spiritual authority the Lord had placed over me. I avoided going to him in confidence and submitting to his covering and oversight in the matter. The appeal of my own ministry became a distraction that could have caused many people so much pain.

When the true time came for me to move out, I immediately shared my plans with my pastor. I gave him a one-year notice of my intentions, and I ultimately remained under his pastorate for two more years serving faithfully wherever I was needed.

It took five years before we started John 3:16 Ministries[19]. In those precious interim years, God dealt with issues of my character. He molded me to trust Him and not just to try and imitate the façade of what I thought a pastor should be.

Had I started a church in 1987, I would have destroyed many lives, including my own and my families'. I would have lost the respect of the ministry community. It is highly possible that the church would be closed in failure. Rather than writing this book, I would probably be trying to overcome self-inflicted issues in a church that would have been dysfunctional from the onset. I truly was not ready in 1987.

In 1992, when my wife and I stepped out in faith (and in order) to establish the church, God miraculously began providing for us. Sound equipment was donated. Musical equipment was donated. A van was donated. A 37-passenger bus was donated. Even the building was provided miraculously. I am thankful that no pastor I've ever served under can accuse us of being deceptive in our quest to obey the Lord.

---

[19] John 3:16 Ministries was the original name of our church.

Distractions will appeal to your carnal appetite. They will appear to be easy roads. At times they will appear to be God sent. Distractions will be pleasant for food, pleasant to the eyes, and give you the impression that you will be wise (Genesis 3:6; First John 2:16).

The pathway of the Lord may seem difficult. Be settled in your spirit that you will pay whatever price is necessary to attain your God given destiny. The cross is very painful, but it is the only way to obtain a ministry or to fulfill a calling that functions in resurrection power (Matthew 16:24). To avoid distraction you must have a clear vision of your purpose, and be willing to pay the price to obtain it.

And David said, What have I now done? Is there not a cause? (1Samuel 17:29)

David asked his brother two significant questions. The first was more of a challenge than a defense. By asking "What have I now done?' he challenged Eliab to show that he was out of order. This was quickly followed up with, "Is there not a cause?" Is there not an issue that needs attention? David instinctively knew that the problem was not between him and his brother, but rather between Israel and the Philistines. Had he allowed himself to be drawn into Eliab's taunts, he may have missed his date with Goliath.

How often have we quoted, "*Where there is no vision, the people perish...*" (Proverbs 29:18)? How often have we failed to consider the last part of this passage, "*...but he that keepeth the law, happy is he*"?

You will perish, or cast off restraint without a vision. Notice that vision is effective within the boundaries of divine law. When I speak of the law, I am not speaking of religious legalism. I am speaking about boundaries created by discipline.

An unfocused, visionless person can be swayed in any direction at any time. The bible has several definitions for these people. They are tossed to and fro by every wind of doctrine (Ephesians 4:14). They are double-minded in all their ways (James 1:8). They are often the target of jokes (Proverbs 14:18). They are gullible (Proverbs 14:15; Romans 16:18).

The Hebrew word used in Proverbs 29:18 for 'keepeth' is *shamar*. It means to guard and protect. The word translated 'law' is *towrah*, which is a precept or a statute. In context, as it is used in this passage, it could also be translated '*instruction*'.

The instructions, precepts or statutes that govern your life must be guarded. *You cannot afford to let every new religious fad, doctrine or philosophy change your direction.* You must have a foundation from which all your decisions are made. A person that has no clue as to what they believe, or why they believe it, can be easily misled. The person without a plan for their life is subject to the manipulation of other agendas. The promise of the Word of God is that you will never fall, be misled or manipulated if you make your calling and election sure (2Peter 1:10).

Principle 7

Keep Your Enthusiasm

ENTHUSIASM AND TENACITY EXCITES EVERYBODY. YOUR ATTITUDE IS **90%** OF YOUR SUCCESS OR FAILURE. KEEP AN ENTHUSIASTIC AND ENERGETIC ATTITUDE AND YOUR MESSAGE WILL GET INTO THE HANDS OF THE RIGHT PEOPLE.

And he turned from him toward another, and spake after the same manner: and the people answered him again after the former manner. And when the words were heard which David spake, they rehearsed them before Saul: and he sent for him. (1Samuel 17:30,31)

David did not allow Eliab's attitude to deter him. In some ways he ignored him. The bible says that *he turned from him toward another.*

129

Sometimes when a person fails to hear truth, rather than argue with him, go to those who will hear it. It is difficult to convince a person who has already set himself against you.

Enthusiasm and tenacity are the fuel that keeps you moving towards your destiny. The Webster's New Collegiate Dictionary[20] reveals a very interesting definition of *enthusiasm*.

Enthusiasm is first described as a belief in special revelations of the Holy Spirit. Scripture tells us that the Holy Spirit will guide us into all truth, and show us things to come (John 16:13). He will show you things from the Lord Jesus Christ (John 16:14). A revelation from the Lord is a life changing experience.

God began birthing a revelation of victory over the Philistines in David's heart. He could see Goliath defeated and Israel victorious. But realize, the path to that victory had the potential of costing David his life.

> ... *neither will I offer burnt offerings unto the LORD my God of that which doth cost me nothing... (2Samuel 24:24)*

True revelation from the Lord is costly. I am not impressed by those who get excited about revelations that cost them nothing. I submit to you that many in the church walk in *hyped up information*, rather than Holy Spirit led revelation. A revelation from the Lord could cost you everything you have. Friends, money, possessions and

---

[20] *Webster's New Collegiate Dictionary* Copyright © 1981 by G. & C. Merriam Co.

family could be the price you pay for walking in a true revelation of the Lord. Can you remain excited under those circumstances?

Second, enthusiasm is also described as *religious fanaticism*. No one wants to be labeled a fanatic. We all want to appear normal. But, enthusiasm may require that you step outside the norm. We have made fanaticism a negative thing, yet we admire those whose fanatic ways resulted in great victories.

Some considered Thomas Edison a fanatic because of his endless experiments with the incandescent light. The Wright brothers were laughed at because they believed they could fly. Madame C.J. Walker dared to believe that a black woman, in the early 1900's could own and operate a beauty care products empire. A.G. Gaston developed a black-owned insurance corporation that still impacts Birmingham, Alabama today. During their quest for success, they risked their money, reputation and personal possessions to achieve their goals. Some of their family and friends saw them as fanatics. In the midst of great odds, they never lost their enthusiasm.

A few years ago I was asked to be the keynote speaker at an event. They had chosen for a theme, WE ARE MAKING HISTORY NOW. As I meditated on this topic, I became aware that those who are making history now are not necessarily the most popular person in the crowd. We celebrate great people of the past as historical icons, yet we fail to remember the pain and suffering they often endured creating that history.

David had every reason to give up. He was a young kid of about sixteen or seventeen years old. He had no battle experience. His oldest brother, and possibly his other brothers were against him. Yet, he never lost his enthusiasm.

> *And when the words were heard which David spake, they rehearsed them before Saul: and he sent for him. And David said to Saul, Let no man's heart fail because of him; thy servant will go and fight with this Philistine. And Saul said to David, Thou art not able to go against this Philistine to fight with him: for thou art but a youth, and he a man of war from his youth. (1 Samuel 17:31-33)*

When people see that you are willing to risk everything to achieve your goal, they are more apt to embrace your vision. It wasn't long before David's story made it to King Saul who had fretted forty days in the palace trying to figure out a way to defeat the Philistines. He had offered his daughter, money and a tax-free life, and yet they were still in the same place.

I imagine he was thrilled to hear that someone was willing to confront Goliath. But it must have come as a shock for him to see this little kid, David, being ushered into his presence. Saul probably resigned himself to imminent defeat. Yet David was bold and confident. He told Saul to take heart. He was ready and willing to take on the giant. Saul's response exposed his fearful heart. "You are just a kid! This Goliath guy is a trained warrior! He has been wiping out little runts like you before you were born!"[21]

David wasn't deterred. He exhibited another trait of enthusiasm. Enthusiasm causes you to view obstacles as opportunities. Your giants become another learning experience in your path to success. David saw the Philistine giant as a simple easily defeatable animal.

> *And David said unto Saul, Thy servant kept his father's sheep, and there came a lion, and a bear, and took a lamb out of the flock: And I went out after him, and smote him, and delivered it out of his mouth: and when he arose against me, I caught him by his beard, and smote him, and slew him. Thy servant slew both the lion and the bear: and this uncircumcised Philistine shall be as one of them, seeing he hath defied the armies of the living God. David said moreover, The LORD that delivered me out of the paw of the lion, and out of the paw of the bear, he will deliver me out of the hand of this Philistine. And Saul said unto David, Go, and the LORD be with thee. (1 Samuel 17:34-37)*

Israel saw Goliath as a big problem. David saw Goliath as a big target. Israel ran from him, and David ran to him. How you view your giants will determine your success. You will almost always encounter a giant in your quest for victory. Giants will only guard land that is valuable. Their presence will try to intimidate you and keep you from the place flowing with milk, honey and great clusters of grapes.

---

[21] The Apostle Tim Kurtz translation of 1Samuel 17:33

How you view yourself can affect your enthusiasm.

And there we saw the giants, the sons of Anak, which come of the giants: and we were in our own sight as grasshoppers, and so we were in their sight. (Numbers 13:33)

After their miraculous deliverance from Egypt, Israel finally made it to the borders of their promise land. Moses sent spies ahead to check it out. After forty days, they returned with the tangible proof that Canaan was exactly as God had promised. But, to them there was a problem.

Although the land had the provision they were promised, it also was filled with giants that were intimidating to Israel. They saw themselves as grasshoppers, and assumed the giants saw them the same way. This poor view of themselves caused them to wander forty years in the wilderness.

After forty years Israel had another opportunity to enter into their land of promise. Joshua sent out two spies to check out the land. The spies were protected by Rahab, a harlot that lived on the walls of Jericho. She revealed what the giants were thinking forty years before.

And [Rahab] said unto the men, I know that the LORD hath given you the land, and that your terror is fallen upon us, and that all the inhabitants of the land faint because of you. For we have heard how the LORD dried up the water of the Red sea for you, when ye came out of Egypt; and what ye did unto the two kings of the Amorites, that were on

the other side Jordan, Sihon and Og, whom ye utterly destroyed. <u>And as</u>
<u>*soon as we had heard these things, our hearts did melt, neither did there*</u>
<u>*remain any more courage in any man, because of you*</u>*: for the LORD your*
God, he is God in heaven above, and in earth beneath. (Joshua 2:9-11)

Did the giants see Israel as grasshoppers? Absolutely not, in fact, the giants were afraid of them. Their hearts melted anticipating Israel's invasion. It must have been a relief for them to see Israel retreat into the wilderness.

Fear will cause you to lose your enthusiasm. You begin to lose the moment you see your perceived shortcomings as greater than God's promises to you. Settle it in your heart right now that whatever God has promised you, He is able to perform (Romans 4:21). Never lose your enthusiasm.

Chapter 12

Principle 8

Use What God Gives You

WHATEVER GOD USES TO PREPARE YOU IS SUFFICIENT FOR REACHING YOUR DESTINY

Try to imagine what was going through Saul's mind. For forty days his army had been verbally defeated by the Philistine giant. He had offered great rewards to anyone who would defeat Goliath, but had no takers. Now he gets word that there was one willing to confront the enemy, and in comes this little teenage kid.

I suspect that Saul was ready to sign the surrender papers. His best warriors did not have the courage to fight Goliath, and he is now looking at some young whippersnapper wanting the opportunity. As he looked at David, he probably saw his honor being diminished. He instinctively knew that Goliath would consider the presence of David as a joke. The great king Saul had an army of wimps, and is sending out a kid to do a man's job. All of this may be the reason Saul tried to dress David up in his armor. Maybe he felt David would look more 'military' in an armored suit.

> *And Saul armed David with his armour, and he put an helmet of brass upon his head; also he armed him with a coat of mail. And David girded his sword upon his armour, and he assayed to go; for he had not proved it. And David said unto Saul, I cannot go with these; for I have not proved them. And David put them off him. (1 Samuel 17:38,39)*

Saul reluctantly agreed to let David go into this battle (1Samuel 17:38-39). Now this kid had the audacity to turn down the king's armor.

David was diplomatic in his approach. "King Saul", he said, "I haven't had the opportunity to try this great stuff out, so if you don't mind I'll use what I already have." In other words, David tactfully told Saul that he wasn't about to use armor that hadn't worked for him. Saul's armor had not produced a victory for him or his army, yet he tried to send David to battle in it. *Never use tools that have failed to work for someone else.*

Everyday you are being prepared for tomorrow's battles. Whatever you face now is the training you need to strengthen you for your destiny.

As you move forward, you will find that you will have multitudes of advisors. They will offer you a game plan they claim to be a guaranteed winner. People will offer you their polished armor to use in battles they are afraid to fight. This is why you must know the strategy of the Lord in everything you do.

This is the heart of effective ministry. You must have a specific strategy from the Lord, to use in specific battles.

Ministry is serving. You need a divine strategy to serve God's purposes. The issue before David was not the death of Goliath – it was the victory of Israel, and Goliath was a hindrance to that victory.

David's training was in the sheep fields of his daddy. His courage was molded in his battles with the lion and the bear. He was familiar with his weapon of choice - a simple slingshot. This was the way he would fight Goliath.

One day you may realize that it was your days as an usher that taught you how to relate to all kinds of people. You may find that a seemingly dead-end job was used by God to show you vital information you needed to start a business. It may be a personal tragic loss that God uses to train you to lead many out of adversity. Whatever the case may be, the Lord will train you so that you can be effective in your calling, purpose and ministry.

...but they measuring themselves by themselves, and comparing themselves among themselves, are not wise. (2Corinthians 10:12)

You cannot afford to look at another person to determine your self worth. David could have become intimidated by what appeared to be older, stronger and more capable men. But he knew what was in him. He was confident of his own God given abilities. Never compare yourself with another.

Just because something hasn't been done, doesn't mean it can't be done. Think about this for a moment. There wasn't an automobile before someone invented it. There wasn't a fax machine before someone invented it. There wasn't a computer before someone invented it. Of course your calling, purpose and ministry won't exist until you begin. What you have to offer only exists in you. Only you can fulfill your purpose. The picture you have in your spirit was given by God to you alone.

Israel had been verbally defeated by the Philistines for forty days. When David arrived on the scene, there was no indication that anything was about to change. He could have simply said nothing could be done because nothing had been done.

Never compare the potential of your future by your present circumstances. If you have dreams of great financial wealth, and you are currently on welfare, your circumstances can change. You have the ability to step out of any rut you may be in. A rut is repeating the same failures at a deeper level. The longer you stay on the same path of failure, the more comfortable your failure will become to you.

I often teach, "IF YOU ALWAYS DO WHAT YOU ALWAYS DID - YOU'LL ALWAYS GET WHAT YOU ALWAYS GOT!" The only way to change tomorrow is by doing something different today.

Chapter 13

Principle 9

Commit to Overcome All Obstacles

YOU WILL FACE GIANTS AND ENCOUNTER ROADBLOCKS. YOU MUST HAVE CONFIDENCE AND COURAGE IN THE FACE OF YOUR ENEMIES AND OBSTACLES.

> *And he took his staff in his hand, and chose him five smooth stones out of the brook, and put them in a shepherd's bag which he had, even in a scrip; and his sling was in his hand: and he drew near to the Philistine. (1Samuel 17:40)*

The hour of truth is here. The greatest test you will face prior to achieving anything of greatness is coming face to face with the giant. Your greatest hurdle will come when you are confronted with a seemingly insurmountable roadblock.

It is important that you recognize the difference between a giant and a roadblock. Each represents a unique learning experience. This is the place where many throw in the towel, not realizing that this is the place where your victory is birthed.

Let's first look at a roadblock. You are traveling towards a certain destination. You have a specific time you need to arrive. You are in an unknown area. You regularly check your map to insure that you are moving in the right direction.

Your momentum is strong. Everything is coming together. All the landmarks indicated on your map verify you are on the right road. You are right on schedule. Suddenly, in front of you is a sign reading 'ROAD CLOSED'. This is no doubt an unexpected roadblock. You must take an alternate route in order to reach your destination. Your only other choice is to give up or turn back. The path you were on is no longer available. You must make some drastic changes. This is the effect a roadblock has on your desire to accomplish a specific goal.

THE STORY OF THE WIFE OF MY FRIEND JOHN

A roadblock may be the loss of a job, a serious illness, a broken relationship, the betrayal of a friend or an unexpected death. Each reflects a point where a vision may be changed or ended.

John had a vision for an urban ministry. He was passionate about his desire to help those trapped in inner city blight. He would tell his story wherever he had the opportunity. I personally helped him to establish his corporate papers, and soon others began to embrace his vision.

A local church had an old condemned two-story brick house in the heart of one of the inner city areas. Upon hearing his vision, they donated the house to him for his ministry. John immediately went to work seeking donations for materials and labor to renovate this old building. Even though it was structurally sound, the renovation needs seemed insurmountable.

Over a period of about two years, this once horrible eyesore began to take on new life. Much of the beautiful woodwork was restored. A lovely kitchen was installed. The circular stairwell became the center of attraction in the foyer. On several occasions, my wife and I would visit them in their home and simply marvel at how God miraculously provided money, labor and materials to this visionary. We were literally in tears on the day that the first phase of his dream became reality, and this building was open for ministry. The Open House celebration was visited by people from all walks of life.

Throughout the renovation process, John's wife was right by his side supporting his vision. She was a constant encouragement to him during times that it seemed all was lost. Although John undoubtedly was the driving force behind the work, she was a tremendous asset that fueled his engines of progress. They each shared in this great vision.

Then it happened. Early Thanksgiving morning we received a call. My friend John, who had worked so hard, had a massive heart attack.

My wife and I rushed to the hospital praying all the way, but when we arrived we were told the horrible news that he was dead.

It wasn't until several weeks later that it sank in that John's dream for an urban ministry was seemingly cut short by his untimely death. Many expected his wife to close the ministry. After all, her involvement in the day-to-day operations had been minimal. No one would have blamed her for walking away.

After a few months of considering her options, this brave woman did the unexpected. She set her eyes on the original vision held by her husband, John. His unexpected death was an almost insurmountable roadblock. She had no experience running social programs or writing grants. The one thing she had was the desire to see her husband's dream remain alive.

She gathered a board of advisors and workers that were crucial to the development of the ministry. Slowly, small programs were instituted in the house. Single women with children were provided temporary housing. Clothing was being distributed, and funds were beginning to trickle in.

It wasn't long before her efforts attracted the attention of a woman who had a heart to operate a ministry such as they were developing. It became obvious that she was the perfect person to assume the oversight of the ministry. The vision my friend John had was kept alive because his wife understood that his death was a roadblock not a conclusion. His death meant the path changed, not the destination. Her desire was simply to see her husband's dream live on.

God's calling on us requires that our fruit remains, even after we are gone (John 15:16). Your calling may be birthed out of your skills and passions. Your purpose will challenge the unmet needs you see. Your ultimate ministry, the strategy God gives you must live on beyond you.

A roadblock is an inanimate obstacle. It has no feelings. It cannot speak to you. It may temporarily stop you and it may present you with the potential of complete loss. So what do you do when faced with a roadblock? You choose another direction to your destination.

John's wife knew that the goal was an effective inner city ministry. His sudden death was a clear roadblock. He wasn't stricken with an illness that may have allowed him to recuperate and possibly continue his work. He was dead. Therefore the only way to accomplish the vision was to take a different route. She had to find other allies and supporters to make his dream live on. I commend her for being willing to turn loose the reigns of the ministry to the person who would keep it alive.

As you pursue your calling, purpose or ministry, you can't allow roadblocks to stop you. Keep your eyes on your destination. Be ready and willing to consider other options.

There may turn out to be some positive benefits resulting from a roadblock. You may find that it will expose some people who should not be with you. There may be times when you find that a roadblock will force you to eliminate things that will hinder your work.

Regardless, always remember that the roadblock is only a sign to take a new direction. It does not mean you are to stop.

GIANTS

David didn't face a roadblock, he faced a giant. Giants are living beings. Giants can talk. Even though they are large and intimidating in size, it is their verbal threats that strike fear in most of us. When David arrived, Goliath began to ridicule him. There are five traits exhibited by the giants you face.

> And the Philistine came on and drew near unto David; and the man that bare the shield went before him. (1Samuel 17:41)

First, the giant had a man bearing his shield. Giants, as large as they are, rarely fight alone. He sent the man with his shield before him. If someone had made a surprise attack, the shield bearer would most likely have received the first blow.

> And when the Philistine looked about, and saw David, he disdained him: for he was but a youth, and ruddy, and of a fair countenance. (1Samuel 17:42)

Second, giants look upon others with disdain. They see everyone as insignificant. Consequently they place no value on those they dislike. Giants will try and make you feel worthless.

> And the Philistine said unto David, Am I a dog, that thou comest to me with staves?...(1Samuel 17:43)

Third, giants will try to make you feel that your weapons of war are worthless against them. They will ridicule your calling. They will declare your purpose as meaningless. They will say your ministry is futile.

And the Philistine cursed David by his gods. (1Samuel 17:43)

Fourth, giants will attempt to use their religious belief system against you. Their desire is to try and make their beliefs seem more viable than yours. True believers are often taunted by liberal religious ideologies who embrace sinful lifestyles, and mock holiness as intolerance.

And the Philistine said to David, Come to me, and I will give thy flesh unto the fowls of the air, and to the beasts of the field. (1Samuel 17:44)

Fifth, giants will try to intimidate you. They will try and strike fear in your heart. They attempt to make you believe that all is lost. They try and make their hopes for victory seem factual. They know that what you see and hear has the potential to paralyze you.

THE VOICE AND SIZE OF THE GIANT

The size of the giant can frighten and emotionally paralyze you, yet the greatest weapon the giant has is his mouth. They use intimidation and fear. The voice of the giant can be heard whenever you get close to your vision. Here are some of his familiar threats.

You don't have enough money to do this!

We've always done it this way!

You've never done this before!

Why embarrass yourself with failure!

You're a woman!

You're too old for this type of work!

You don't have enough education!

The people will not support you!

The moment you hear these statements, you should know that you may be facing a giant and there is only one solution, *Kill him! Don't negotiate with him. Don't give him the chance to recuperate and as soon as he is down – decapitate him.* Giants will always fall before anyone who is confident of their mission. This may be hard for some to accept. It seems brutal. After all, aren't we Christians suppose to be loving and kind?

> *From that time forth began Jesus to show unto his disciples, how that he must go unto Jerusalem, and suffer many things of the elders and chief priests and scribes, and be killed, and be raised again the third day. Then Peter took him, and began to rebuke him, saying, Be it far from thee, Lord: this shall not be unto thee. BUT HE TURNED, AND SAID UNTO PETER, GET THEE BEHIND ME, SATAN: thou art an offence unto me: for thou savourest not the things that be of God, but those that be of men. (Matthew 16:22)*

Just prior to this hard rebuke from Jesus, Peter had declared Jesus to be the Christ, Son of the Living God. Yet, a few moments later he was being called satan.

Jesus exhibited the attitude you must have against *any spirit* that tries to undermine God's plan for your life. Evil and demonic spirits use people to do their work. Inevitably when you deal with evil, you are often in front of a human being. Jesus was not attacking Peter per se. Even thought Jesus addressed Peter, He was not making Peter satan. Jesus was confronting the spirit of satan that was influencing Peter. Jesus knew that He had to go to the cross and Peter's words were a reflection of satan's attempt to distract and detour Him.

The giants you face may not have the physical size of Goliath, but you have to be able to discern its voice. What is said can be the voice of a giant guised as a close friend or acquaintance. At times it may require a rebuke, but most often it demands that you remain steadfast in your purpose.

God has called me to address the values and structure of the New Testament Church. This requires a shift in how we view the church. I am called to build a prototype church that embraces and activates first century values and structure. This book will not detail every aspect of my purpose, but suffice it to say, it at times is a daunting task.

In pursuit of my purpose, at times I encounter those who either don't understand or are opposed to what I teach. Some are passive, choosing to sit on the sidelines while others are quite vocal in their opposition. God has spiritually and emotionally equipped me to handle these situations. However, I was nearly blindsided when a person who I thought fully supported what I had been teaching confronted me with this statement, "What have you ever accomplished?" The bluntness and sarcasm in their voice stunned me.

I immediately thought of Jesus' rebuke of Peter. I realized that I was hearing the voice of satan through that person. The challenge to what I have accomplished struck an historical nerve in me. During my life I have struggled with completing projects and goals. I have made a concentrated effort to end this trait by surrounding myself with counselors and mentors who constantly challenge me. The person who made the statement had no knowledge of what I was dealing with, but satan knew it and used them to attack me. It was the voice of the giant attempting to thwart my ministry work. I did not rebuke the person like Jesus did Peter, but I definitely took note of the challenge.

Physically, the person was not a giant, but there was clearly a spiritual giant seeking to stop me. It was a giant of my own past taunting me. This challenge motivated me to stay the course, and above all destroy the giant.

What giants do you face? Is it a popular religious belief system? Is it massive public opinion that contradicts what the Lord is showing you? Is it long held traditions? Is it a close well-meaning friend that is opposed to what you believe your calling to be? Such was the case with Peter.

Physically, Peter was not a giant, but his words that he thought was a protective rebuke reflected the voice of a giant trying to fluster Jesus. People who are close to you often speak freely. I seriously doubt if Peter meant any harm, but his lack of discernment was subtly[22] used by satan to come after Jesus. That is why Jesus sharply rebuked the *influencing spirit of satan.* Peter just happened to be the vessel the devil had used.

Neither give place to the devil. (Ephesians 4:27)

You cannot afford to allow satan any room to function against you. You must be firm in your purpose and your stance in the face of the enemy.

> *Then said David to the Philistine, Thou comest to me with a sword, and with a spear, and with a shield: but I come to thee in the name of the LORD of hosts, the God of the armies of Israel, whom thou hast defied. This day will the LORD deliver thee into mine hand; and I will smite thee, and take thine head from thee; and I will give the carcases of the host of the Philistines this day unto the fowls of the air, and to the wild beasts of the earth; that all the earth may know that there is a God in Israel. And all this assembly shall know that the LORD saveth not with sword and spear: for the battle is the Lord's, and he will give you into our hands (1Samuel 17:45-47)*

David made his position clear. He knew that his relationship with the Lord guaranteed his victory. He knew that Goliath was the

---

[22] Genesis 3:1

obstacle to Israel's victory over the Philistines. He wasn't about to try and talk Goliath into surrendering. David knew that Goliath had to die. Goliath represented the spirit that opposes divine destiny.

The devil will attempt to oppose you using the same tactics as Goliath. You may be threatened by people who appear to be more affluent and successful than you. They may have no qualms about letting you know their self-assumed superiority, and may take pride in publicly trying to humiliate you.

You may find yourself confronted with the giant of your own pride. Previous successes can be magnified in your own mind and cause you to shift your faith from God to your own abilities. This becomes an open door for a satanic giant to enter.

You cannot negotiate with the giant of pride. You need the five stones of faith, humility, submission to authority, trust in the Word of God and daily prayer. Go forth with the slingshot of the Holy Ghost and kill the giant of pride. It has to die. You may be facing a giant of debt and poverty. You may feel intimidated by your financial woes. You cannot negotiate with these giants. You must gather up your five stones called tithes, offerings, diligence, faithfulness and obedience and go forth with the sling of the Holy Ghost and kill the giant of poverty and debt.

And it came to pass, when the Philistine arose, and came and drew nigh to meet David, that David hasted, and ran toward the army to meet the Philistine. (1 Samuel 17:48)

Whatever giant you are facing, you must run towards him fully intending to destroy him. You must be ready to revenge any disobedience whenever it manifests (2Corinthians 10:6).

And David put his hand in his bag, and took thence a stone, and slang it, and smote the Philistine in his forehead, that the stone sunk into his forehead; and he fell upon his face to the earth. So David prevailed over the Philistine with a sling and with a stone, and smote the Philistine, and slew him; but there was no sword in the hand of David. Therefore David ran, and stood upon the Philistine, and took his sword, and drew it out of the sheath thereof, and slew him, and cut off his head therewith. And when the Philistines saw their champion was dead, they fled. (1Samuel 17:49-51)

David's first blow against Goliath was on target. His smooth stone found its mark in the forehead of the giant.

I find it interesting that Goliath was struck in the forehead. The forehead is a symbol of the *thought processes*. In Deuteronomy 6:8, Israel was told to know the law so well that it would be as though it were bound to their foreheads. The Apostle Paul told the Ephesians to put on the helmet of salvation. A helmet protects the head – the thinking center. Some helmets were specifically designed to protect the forehead.

For it is written, I will destroy the wisdom of the wise, and will bring to nothing the understanding of the prudent. Where is the wise? where is the

scribe? where is the disputer of this world? hath not God made foolish the
wisdom of this world? (1Corinthians 1:19,20)

Goliath's forehead could represent a type of worldly wisdom. It is the wisdom based on human strength and power. It is the wisdom that attempts to intimidate and take advantage of others. It was here that David's stone found its mark. With one blow, the wisdom of the world came tumbling down.

David's next act is one that we often overlook. He wasn't satisfied with Goliath being knocked cold by the rock. He wanted to make sure that the giant never had another opportunity to taunt Israel again. He cut off Goliath's head. The remarkable thing is, that several days later, David was still carrying the head of Goliath around with him (1Samuel 17:54-58). The head of the giant was a graphic reminder to all Israel that the enemy had been defeated.

And they overcame him by the blood of the Lamb, and by the word of
their testimony; and they loved not their lives unto the death. (Revelation
12:11)

Our trophies are exhibited through our victorious testimonies. When a former crack addict testifies of deliverance, it is proof that the head of the enemy has been taken. When an alcoholic testifies that the bondage of drinking has been broken, it is proof that the head of the enemy has been taken. When those in deep debt have been made financially free, it is proof that the head of the giant has been taken.

We cannot be afraid to carry the trophy of our victories so that others can see the power of the Lord.

Principle 10
Keep Your Eyes On The Goal

KILLING YOUR GIANT OPENS THE DOOR TO YOUR NEXT LEVEL. DON'T BE DETERRED BY JEALOUSY. RESPECT IS THE SPIRIT OF AUTHORITY.

Much of this book so far has dealt with David and his confrontation with Goliath. Now Goliath is dead, and we can get back to the real purpose of David's life. Samuel anointed David to be king, not to defeat Goliath. The giant was the key to David's next level. Had he failed against Goliath, he would have never made it to the throne.

After killing Goliath, Saul brought David to the palace and would not let him go home to his father's house (1Samuel 18:2). This is when God began to introduce David to the inner workings of the palace. Saul set David over the men of war, and he was accepted in the sight of all the people and the servants. It was a time that he became a close friend of Jonathan, Saul's son. In the back of his mind, I am sure that David remembered Samuel anointing him for Saul's job, but the bible says that he behaved himself wisely (1Samuel 18:5).

> *And Moses was learned in all the wisdom of the Egyptians, and was mighty in words and in deeds. (Acts 7:22)*

> *For it was so, when Jezebel cut off the prophets of the LORD, that Obadiah took an hundred prophets, and hid them by fifty in a cave, and fed them with bread and water. (1Kings 18:4)*

I love the strategies of the Lord. When He wanted to prepare a deliverer for Israel, He had Moses trained in Pharaoh's house. Moses was educated by the very people he would one day overthrow. When Jezebel was slaughtering the prophets of the Lord, God used Obadiah, a governor in her household to hide fifty of the prophets in a cave, and feed them with bread and water most likely from Ahab's and Jezzie's pantry. So when God determined to raise David up to be king He orchestrated David's entrance into the palace to serve the one he would replace. God will put you in the right place to see the right things. It is how you handle yourself during this process that is critical to your future.

> *And it came to pass as they came, when David was returned from the slaughter of the Philistine, that the women came out of all cities of Israel, singing and dancing, to meet king Saul, with tabrets, with joy, and with instruments of music. and the women answered one another as they*

played, and said, Saul hath slain his thousands, and David his ten thousands. and Saul was very wroth, and the saying displeased him; and he said, They have ascribed unto David ten thousands, and to me they have ascribed but thousands: and what can he have more but the kingdom? And Saul eyed David from that day and forward. (1Samuel 18:6-9)

Whenever you achieve promotion, persecution is close by. David's success brought him popularity among the people but it also attracted the jealousy of the king.

In chapter four you learned that *responsibility* is the foundation of confidence. I now add that *respect* is the *spirit of authority*. Your revelation is the strength of your authority, but failure to understand the significance of respecting others will undermine any true authority you could have.

Throughout his life, David instinctively knew how to respect those in authority. Three times scripture says that David behaved himself wisely. This caused Saul to fear David and to become his enemy (1Samuel 18:5; 18:14; 18:15; 18:30).

A critical point in your ministry will be when you have the opportunity to flaunt your successes. The women sang that Saul killed his thousands but David his ten thousands. David never allowed their accolades to go to his head. He still honored Saul as the king.

Unfortunately Saul missed the whole issue. If he had defeated a thousand, and David had defeated ten thousand, then together they defeated eleven thousand. Instead, he felt the numbers reflected his self worth.

Successful people know that the exterior façade does not truly reflect what is on the inside. At this point in his life, David was not impressed by the numbers. He did what he had to do and the numbers spoke for themselves.

Several years ago, I heard a man say, *"What you think about me -- is none of my business!"* Saul hated David. David behaved himself wisely. Your character, good or bad, is reflected in how you respond to those who dislike you. If someone doesn't like you because of your success, let that be their problem, not yours.

Another example is Joseph.

After being sold into slavery by his brothers, being falsely accused by his slave master's wife, years languishing in prison, and being forgotten by the one he ministered to in prison, Joseph was elevated to second in command in Egypt. In the pinnacle of his life he came face to face with those who had caused him so much pain – his own brothers. This was an opportunity for pay back. He had the authority to punish them with or without cause, but he chose to bless and provide for them. He understood the trajectory of his life had a purpose that would have been cut short by revenge (Genesis 50:20).

David's Sin

And David's heart smote him after that he had numbered the people. And David said unto the LORD, I have sinned greatly in that I have done: and now, I beseech thee, O LORD, take away the iniquity of thy servant; for I have done very foolishly. (2Samuel 24:10)

Later in life, David took a census of the people. Theologians are conflicted as to why this act was so wrong. Historically, there had been other census taken without any negative impact. The primary conclusion is that David took this census in an act of pride. It is surmised that he wanted the census to bolster his image. This mistake that cost seventy thousand lives in three days (2Samuel 24:15).

When you value yourself by external things it reveals two significant things: your lack of trust in God, and the lack of respect for those around you. You cannot trust God and depend on the strength of man at the same time. Large numbers do not impress God. Military might does not frighten Him. Only faith in His Word moves Him.

When you value yourself by external things you potentially can harm those who look to you for direction. You will tend to invest more in your image than your character. You will find yourself migrating to anything that makes you look good to the public. When pride causes you to entrust your value in exterior things, you are more apt to hurt those around you for the sake of your image. It is the Hollywood mentality.

The business world is filled with people who climbed the ladder of worldly success on the backs of other people. I know people who took pride in crushing people in their quest for the top. I have seen these same people's lives end up in shambles. I am saddened by churches that dis-fellowship individuals because they supposedly brought a *reproach* upon the church. The truth is that they often kick people out because they embarrassed the 'holier than reality' image of the church. No one can bring a reproach upon the church. Why? We all have sinned and fallen short of God's glory (Romans 3:23; 5:12). I don't believe scripture validates us throwing people out of the church.

Matthew 18:17 has been misinterpreted for this reason. When a brother is at fault, and refuses to hear truth from the church, Jesus said let him BE TO YOU as a heathen and a publican. In other words, you should still try to win him (Matthew 18:15), but rather than dealing with a brother, you are dealing with one who is like a heathen and publican. You don't minister to a brother in the Lord the same way you minister to a sinner.

If a member sins, we deal with the sin and seek to restore them. The process may be long and arduous, but to dis-fellowship them is, in my opinion, an act of religious arrogance and pride.

I believe in holiness (Hebrews 12:14). I believe in discipline and correction when it is required (2Timothy 4:2). I also believe in restoring those that have sinned against me, or that have fallen into error (Galatians 6:1,2).

When you trust in your image rather than your character, you rely on things that can change in a moment. When you hide behind your looks, your money, your car, clothes or home, you set yourself up to be devastated the moment they change. One bad investment and your money could be gone. An accident can destroy your vehicle. Age, illness or accidents can change your looks, and the list goes on. Build a strong character that overrides any exterior possession you may possess.

In his book, THE SEVEN HABITS OF HIGHLY EFFECTIVE PEOPLE[23], Stephen R. Covey outlines our shift from the Character to the Personality Ethic. He states that *character* is rooted in integrity, humility, fidelity, temperance, courage, justice, patience and so on. It is not until these become the fiber of our daily living that we can achieve real success.

On the other hand, because we have shifted to the *Personality Ethic*, success has become more of a fruit of public image, skills and techniques. Many times actions were manipulative and deceptive. Public Relation firms earn millions making reprobates look righteous.

There is a vast difference between the *fruit of the Spirit* (Galatians 5:22-24; Ephesians 5:9) and the *works of the flesh* (Galatians 5:19-21). The production of fruit requires a seed, cultivation and the test of time prior to a harvest. I believe the seed that produces the fruit of the Spirit is the Word of God. You must receive the engrafted Word of God (James 1:21). It has to become a part of us.

Then we need to cultivate ourselves so the Word can grow in us. To cultivate means to prepare the soil by breaking it up, in order to

---

[23] The 7 Habits of Highly Effective People Copyright © 1989 by Stephen R. Covey

foster growth. There are issues in us that need to be broken up in order for the Word to take root and grow in us.

Time is the tester of commitment. Fruit comes with time. It is not instantaneous. In time you will face the weeds of compromise, complacency and corruption. The weeds that choke the Word in you are framed by the works of the flesh. You must commit to righteousness.

Your character is more than your outward image. Don't be moved by those who pat you on the back. Don't change your attitude towards others as you rise to the top. Remember, God resists the proud but gives grace to the humble (James 4:6).

Pride and jealousy will cause you to lose sight of your goal. You may defeat a giant, but if your victory becomes a source of pride you will quickly lose sight of your ultimate goal.

The Conclusion

The Revelation of Who You Are

My wife and I started the church we serve in April of 1992. Week after week we held services believing that God was with us. I remember being amazed that people actually showed up.

In November of 1992, the Lord spoke to me regarding John 3:16 Ministries[24]. He said, *"I've called you to this work. The vision you see is mine".* For the first time, I had a confidence that was unshakable.

Revelation is the basis of authority. It is the key to any successful endeavor.

As a young boy, the prophet Samuel anointed David king in midst of his brothers. For the next thirteen to fifteen years he struggled with lions, bears, giants and even a deranged king.

He hid in caves. He led a group of four hundred misfits (1Samuel 22:1-2), who later became his mighty army (2Samuel 23:8 - 24:39). He led them from victory to victory. It wasn't until David conquered the

---

[24] John 3:16 Ministries was the original name of the church. It has since been changed to New Life Ministries International.

167

unconquerable that a remarkable thing took place in his life (2Samuel 5:7):

And David perceived that the LORD had established him king over Israel, and that he had exalted his kingdom for his people Israel's sake. (2 Samuel 5:12)

David perceived that the Lord had established him king over Israel. He realized that he was actually the king. The Moffatt Translation says that, *David realized that the Eternal had set him to be king over Israel.*

Your calling may alert you to your destiny but it requires process to activate you into it. I once saw a television documentary about some of our recent presidents. It was interesting to note when some of them realized that they were President of the United States.

They had run grueling campaigns. They had spent millions of dollars and expended unimaginable energy in their quest for the White House. They won the election. It was international news. Yet, both Presidents Carter and Ford said they really didn't realize they were president until they entered the Oval Office for the first time. That's when it sank in. It dawned on President Reagan that he was President of the United States when he saw the moving van bringing their furniture into the White House. *Many times our journey towards a goal is so demanding that we miss the time of our arrival.*

There is an African Proverb that says, "It's not what you call me that matters – it is what I answer to". There will be a time when you will receive a revelation from God as to who you really are. People can call you an apostle, prophet or evangelist, but it is not until you embrace who God says you are that you will be effective. You have authority when you are confident of who you are and what you are called to do.

> *Am I not an apostle? am I not free? have I not seen Jesus Christ our Lord? are not ye my work in the Lord? If I be not an apostle unto others, yet doubtless I am to you: for the seal of mine apostleship are ye in the Lord. (1Corinthians 9:1)*

Responsibility is the foundation of authority. Long before Paul asserted his apostleship over the Corinthian church, he had served with Barnabas as an errand boy in the Jerusalem church (Acts 9:26,27; Acts 11:29,30; Acts 12:25). He served in an atmosphere where many doubted him because of his previous lifestyle of persecuting the church.

Now is the time for you to walk in responsibility. Don't try and wait until you are *'doing your calling'*. Be responsible now! You may be anointed to become a worldwide evangelist, but right now you are an usher in your church. Be the best usher your church has. If you work in the nursery, do all you can to make it a state of the art child-care facility.

Don't look for the 'pat on the back'. Expect to be in the background. You are under a Holy Ghost microscope. Your actions today are the seed for your true calling, purpose and ministry tomorrow.

Be faithful. God is looking for faithful servants (Matthew 25:21-23; Hebrews 6:10). Serve wherever you can. On your day of divine promotion, your actions today will produce the fruit of your ministry tomorrow.

Respect is the spirit of authority. For fourteen years after his conversion, Paul submitted himself to other apostles. There is no evidence that he tried to assert himself before God was ready for him (Acts 13:2). Even when there was a dispute regarding the circumcision, he submitted himself to the authority of the Jerusalem church (Acts 15).

Don't get ahead of yourself or God. Submit to your God given spiritual authority. They are people too, and subject to make mistakes which may effect and hurt you. Honor and respect them anyway. The issue is not their actions, but rather your heart.

Floyd Starr once said that, "God can't use discouraged people".[25] You can't afford to let hurt and discouragement become the barometer of your destiny.

Let love be without dissimulation. Abhor that which is evil; cleave to that which is good. (Romans 12:9)

Here is your true challenge. The Word of God instructs us to let love be without dissimulation. The Goodspeed Translation says to 'let

---

[25] An excerpt from *There's No Such Thing As A Bad Boy,* a documentary on the life of Floyd Starr the Founder of Starr Commonwealth Schools in Albion, Michigan

our love be sincere'. Your love and respect must be real. You can't fake this thing.

People will hurt, disappoint, discourage and persecute you. Your love for them can't be lip service because you are trying to get to your calling. It has to be genuine. You have to love people when it costs you money, reputation, friends and honor. Remember, it is the pure in heart that has a true perception of God (Matthew 5:8; 1Peter 1:22).

Finally, *revelation is the basis of authority.* That is to say that once you have a revelation of who you are in the Lord, you can proceed with absolute confidence. Paul asserted his apostolic leadership over the Roman church because he had a clear revelation of who he was. He was confident that the Lord had entrusted him to speak into their lives.

Your revelation of yourself cannot manifest until you have a pure heart. That is why *responsibility and respect* are so important.

God wants you to reach your goal as much as you want to reach it. But He will not entrust the care of his purposes to those who are self-serving and careless. Responsibility demands that you pay the price of commitment to current duties.

Yes, your current duties have more value to the one you are serving. Your future is secondary to their needs (Luke 16:12). That is the price of responsibility.

Respect must remain the heart of all your actions. Think about this. You love your neighbor as you love yourself (Matthew 19:19). If you have to look over your shoulder because you have failed to operate with integrity, it will taint your heart and give you a distorted view of yourself.

If you have spoken ill of your leadership, and complained about their actions, you develop a heart that will view others with suspicion. Your love and respect for others simply reflect your love and respect for yourself.

Now is the time for you to prepare. God has a calling, purpose and ministry for your life. Start where you are. Wait for God's timing. Refuse to become self-centered by believing you are the only one who can do God's will.

Be faithful where you are now. Fulfill your responsibilities with excellence. Expect your destiny to be revealed in your assignment. Remain aware of your environment. God will teach more on your journey than you will learn at your destination.

When you come to an impasse, ask God to help you discern if it is a giant or a roadblock. If it is a roadblock, be willing to take another route to your destination. If it is a giant, kill it. Never lose your enthusiasm. Use your gifts and talents to help others. Above all, never lose sight of your goal.

I believe if you follow this advice, you will successfully achieve your calling, purpose and ministry.

CPSIA information can be obtained at www.ICGtesting.com
Printed in the USA
BVOW02s1525020214

343457BV00009B/142/P